Design and Color in Islamic Architecture

AFGHANISTAN

IRAN

TURKEY

SONIA P. SEHERR-THOSS

HANS C. SEHERR-THOSS *photography*

DONALD N. WILBER *introduction*

SMITHSONIAN INSTITUTION PRESS

CITY OF WASHINGTON

1968

nithsonian Publication 4741
brary of Congress Catalog Card Number 68–28138

signed by Stephen Kraft
twork for endleaves and pages 60 and 64 by Hans C. Seherr-Thoss

inted by the Imprimeries Réunies S.A. Lausanne
Helvetica Press Production

Design
and
Color
in
Islamic
Architecture

Contents

pag

Preface

ISLAMIC DESIGN—in its quest for a new structural expression, new uses of materials, new ways of treating large wall surfaces, and a fresh concept of interior space—has a particular kinship with contemporary architecture.

The Eastern world had a deep respect for tradition; change was evolutionary. Unlike the modern West, the East did not seek today to find tomorrow's solution. Yet the slow pace of the centuries should not be taken as a sign of stagnation. During the seven hundred years covered by this book, Islamic art developed steadily, and in this development, a spirit of creativity prevailed. Originality was never sacrificed to an arid reiteration of the past. Islamic architects sought fresh solutions to the challenges of differing climates and building materials and of diverse aesthetic and social requirements. In their works the virility of the pioneer bridges the intervening ages to bring a vital message to a Western civilization which seeks to free itself from trite " revivals. "

Materials may alter with technical discoveries, but the importance of using a particular material honestly and with a feeling for its potentialities endures. Brick architecture of Iran expresses function at the same time that it explores all the possibilities of its medium. During its great period, this style is an almost perfect statement of the aesthetics of architecture. A discipline that will compromise neither with prettiness nor with the domination of structure is rare—its fulfillment is an inspiration to any era.

Structure, when expressed honestly and powerfully, as in the northeast dome chamber of the Masjid-i-Jami at Isfahan, is exhilarating as well as beautiful. The simple assertion of the towering Gunbad-i-Kabus finds stern conviction in its austerity. The mosaics swirling through the dome at Malatya interpret and dramatize form, as color becomes an integral part of architectural design.

In addition to their general aesthetic interest, Islamic concepts include specific ideas which are pertinent to contemporary design. While we may deplore the atrophying effect of imitation, it would be equally unfortunate to go to the other extreme and reject the wealth of mankind's heritage. Despite cultural, climatic or technical differences, within a broad field of endeavor certain problems recur, and the solutions reached by talented men in another time and place may well be the stimuli which awaken new images.

Moslem builders were particularly concerned with the treatment of large wall surfaces, and they approached this challenge from several viewpoints. In Iran, variations in the method of laying brick created linear patterns and textures; designs were sometimes in quite high relief. Use of a single material for both structure and decoration contributed to the unity of a building, while skillful handling precluded monotony. Some designs evolved naturally from structural features; others were simply geometric panels spotted on a wall as ornament. The textural potentialities of brick (used alone or in conjunction with glazed tile) were fully explored.

The brick decoration has several pleasing features. Since the clay was locally produced, the monument harmonized with the simpler buildings around it. The designs vary with the viewpoint, and fresh images hold the interest. Minor changes in the manner of laying brick, or in the size or shape of the sections, produce surprisingly strong results. Patterns in considerable relief present even greater flexibility as sunlight moves across a surface, stressing first one segment, then another. The juxtaposition of two rough materials (such as the brick and stone of the Muradiye complex at Bursa) is also extremely effective. Here, too, slight modifications in the design enliven details of the façade within a total unity.

Color used in striking accents or in gentle variations—or brilliantly employed to cover an entire monument—played a vital role in Islamic architecture. Glazed brick was first applied in Iran to enhance the brick patterns. The Gunbad-i-Surkh in Maragha (1147-48) presents an early example of color decoration in Iran; here, this new feature was concentrated around the portal. Fifty years later, also in Maragha, the Gunbad-i-Kabud was encased in a decoration of brick and blue tile. Gradually, the proportion of enameled to natural brick or stucco increased, until it culminated in the dazzling tile mosques of Isfahan and Meshed.

In Turkey during the Seljuk period color was occasionally used within the stonework—sometimes as bold patterns and at other times as modulated tones in a color balance arrangement. A tomb tower of the late 13th century in Erzurum illustrates the latter scheme. Although the trend in Turkey was toward strict formality, asymmetry periodically made its appearance, as in the striking panel on the Green Mausoleum at Bursa.

A typical feature of 15th–century Iranian building was the embellishment of great wall surfaces with large-scale patterns in natural and enameled brick—as, for instance, in the *madrasa* at Khargird or the mausoleum of Ahmad-ibn-Allah Hasan in Turbat-i-Shaykh Jam. Even when these buildings are viewed from a considerable distance, color lends vitality to their façades, and it both defines and enhances their architectural forms. Within the edifices, various decorative relationships were developed through repetition and variation of color schemes. A new harmony was thus added to structural rhythms.

The use of shadow lines was another method of breaking the monotony of a flat surface; to obtain this effect, builders employed many devices—moldings, relief panels, brick end plugs, blind arches, raised tracery, and high-relief ornamentation. Shadows come to life in the changing sunlight, stressing new aspects of a design, evoking new interest in it. With these techniques Islamic architects devised an amazing variety of fresh and imaginative ways of handling decoration.

The treatment of space—in terms of both regal proportions and human scaling—had interesting developments in Iran and Turkey.

With due regard for the impressive effect of a religious monument, the Iranians yet achieved a harmonious relationship between the solitary worshiper and the mosque. This was attained largely through the use of small chambers of great height. A soaring dome imparts nobility; at the same time, the proximity of walls in a small area suggests intimacy and seclusion. Other means were also employed to mitigate the lonely effect of space. In contrast to the Christian altar placed within a sanctuary area to which access is restricted, the *mihrab* was always approachable; its beauty was intended to draw the individual from the material to the spiritual world. Passages from the Koran presented familiar texts, yet with the variations in the script they seemed ever novel and fascinating. Detail, especially when related or scaled to man, held the interest and also challenged perception. The pause to understand or appreciate design brings about a personal participation in the structure —a reaction rarely produced by the obvious.

The harsher climate of Turkey precluded the use of open courts for worship, and the entire mosque had to be enclosed. For the congregations of imperial Istanbul, an interior space both vast and majestic had to be developed. Sancta Sophia presented a challenge rather than a solution, for Moslem ritual needs differ basically from the Christian. Sinan, chief architect to Suleyman the

Magnificent, designed great domed chambers whose interior plan was adjusted to Moslem requirements and whose harmonious proportions created repose.

Turkish Islamic architecture differs greatly from that of Afghanistan or Iran, largely because of climate, available building materials and artistic traditions. All three countries, however, make a significant contribution through their sincerity of structural statement, inventiveness of design, appreciation of relief and texture, feeling for proportion and use of color.

This book is not intended as a historical survey of Islamic architecture, nor does it include all the fine monuments in this style. The U.S.S.R., Iraq, Syria, Egypt, India, Pakistan, North Africa and Spain possess outstanding buildings, but space must limit selection. Many Afghan, Iranian and Turkish monuments have been omitted. This is no reflection on their beauty or merit, but came about because other examples were chosen either to show a particular design or use of color, or because they were especially relevant to Western architecture. And it is this pertinence of Islamic architecture and design to contemporary design and aesthetics which is the particular concern of this volume.

Litchfield, Connecticut

SONIA P. SEHERR-THOSS

Acknowledgments

We wish to express our thanks to the many friends and officials who facilitated our trips to Afghanistan, Iran, and Turkey, most especially to Mr. Asad Behroozan who accompanied us for nine weeks through Iran in 1964 and to Mr. Selçuk Batur who acted as photographic assistant and interpreter on our 1966 expedition through Iran and Turkey. We are very grateful to Mr. David Stronach, Director of the British Institute for Persian Studies in Tehran who personally took us to visit the Kharraqan Tomb Towers which he had been studying. Without him that trip would have been almost impossible and, certainly, far less rewarding. Dr. Arthur Upham Pope has advised us on many occasions, placed his library at our disposal, and generously shared his vast knowledge of Iran with us. His enthusiasm stimulated us to undertake this photographic record of Islamic design. Although we are solely responsible for all opinions expressed, we do wish to thank Dr. Donald N. Wilber who kindly read the text and made many very valuable suggestions. The author wishes to thank those who kindly supplied material for the following illustrations: Figure E, Princeton University Press, for the use of material from Wilber, *Architecture of Islamic Iran*, plan 28; Figure G, Dr. Arthur Upham Pope, for the use of material from *Survey of Persian Art*; Figure L, Editions E. de Boccard, for the use of material from Gabriel, *Les monuments turcs d'Anatolie*, I, Figure 54; Figure M, Editions E. de Boccard, for the use of material from Gabriel, *Une capitale turque: Brousse-Bursa*, I, Figure 53; Figure N, Office du Livre, Fribourg, for the use of material from Vogt-Göknil, *Turquie ottomane*, page 88; and Plate 98, Condé Nast Publications, for the use of an H. C. Seherr-Thoss photograph published in the August 1965 issue of *Vogue*.

BLACK SEA

CASPIAN
SEA

U.S.S.R.

ul

Bursa

TURKEY

Kayseri

Tercan • • Erzurum

Konya

Nigde

Tunceli

Malatya

Tabriz

Gunbad-i-Kabus

Maragha

Sultaniya

Gurgan

Bistam

Sangbast

Kharraqan

Tehran

Demavand

Turbat-i-Shaykh Jam

Hisar-
i-Armani

Varamin

Khaf

Khargird

Herat

SYRIA

LEBANON

Natanz

ISRAEL

JORDAN

IRAQ

Isfahan

Nayin

Tabas

AFGHANISTAN

Ashtarjan

Linjan

IRAN

EGYPT

SAUDI ARABIA

RED
SEA

INDIAN OCEAN

List of plates

page

List of figures

Introduction

THE ARCHITECTURE OF the world of Islam has never attracted the attention that it deserves, although its thousands of monuments, erected over many centuries, are to be seen in a band stretching almost halfway around the world. Now that there is an upsurge of interest in this architecture, however, it is worthwhile to attempt to establish some of its basic characteristics—and, first of all, to see why this interest has been so late in appearing.

Europe had come into contact with the lands of the Moslem world in the medieval period: Marco Polo traveled across the Anatolian and Iranian plateaux, on his way to China, before the end of the 13th century, and it was not until 1492 that the last Moslems were expelled from Spain. Later on, merchant traders took the routes of the sea to the East, and were followed by the founders of the colonies of the British, French, Dutch and other empires. In the 16th and 17th centuries explorers, mercenaries, and gentlemen adventurers published their accounts of theking doms of Turkey and Persia, and of teeming India. Wonders were exaggerated, and the unfamiliar held up to scorn. Turkey—a serious military threat to Europe—was regarded with hostility. Some of this hostility was transferred to Islam, since the religion was not understood and Muhammad (Mahomet) was widely thought of as a heathen idol.

The great mosques of Constantinople were clearly visible to the Christian visitors, but entry was forbidden them—as was the case in other Moslem lands. With a few notable exceptions, such as the French jeweler Chardin, who put down a detailed account of the structures of Isfahan as they appeared at the middle of the 17th century, these travelers were not greatly interested in architecture.

These lands became the Orient, a region which encompassed all the lands east—and even south—of the Mediterranean Sea. This Orient was thought of as the realm of the luxurious, picturesque, exotic, and erotic, and this romantic vision was particularly favored in Victorian England, so fascinated by its Indian possession. This so-called Negative Orientalism also conceived of this realm as the home of mystic cults, sensuality, cruelty, dazzling colors, and elaborate ornament.

In Europe men of great talent were revealing the architectural heritages of earlier centuries. At the middle of the 19th century John Ruskin wrote *The Seven Lamps of Architecture* and *The Stones of Venice*. A chapter from the latter book on the nature of Gothic had a great impact, and soon England was flooded with structures in Neo-Gothic style. This style even reached India, where British-built structures at Lahore combined Neo-Gothic with elements from the Indian tradition. In France, Viollet-Le-Duc was popularizing French Gothic and undertaking the restoration of a number of the country's major medieval monuments.

Unfortunately, the earlier architecture of Islam had no such advocates. In India a British governor cleaned up and restored the gardens of the Taj Mahal, while the British authorities undertook an exhaustive survey of the standing structures and of the archeological sites—a survey whose publications never caught the popular eye. In other Moslem lands many stately structures slowly crumbled away, or were robbed of their stones, bricks, and marble for new constructions.

It was not until well into the present century that a number of these lands employed foreign architects and archeologists to explore and to preserve the vestiges of the past: cultural nationalism came on the heels of political nationalism. The first attempts to write the history of Moslem architecture in one or more countries, wisely concentrated on descriptions of structures, supported by facts derived from the Arabic inscriptions on the buildings. Misunderstanding and prejudice remained: Bolus, in *The Influence of Islam*, wrote: " The general outline of the mosque is a constant unvarying factor—a parable of the Moslem intellect which progresses up to a point and then obstinately refuses to advance. Nothing comparable with the stately development of Gothic is to be found in the architectural history of Islam. Had not Muhammad with his own hands helped in erecting the first mosque? What better model could the Moslem then desire? "

The very well-known textbook, *A History of Architecture on the Comparative Method*, by Sir Banister Fletcher, first printed in 1896, has gone through many editions. Fletcher, calling the architecture of Islam Saracenic, placed it among the non-historical styles about which he wrote: " Eastern art presents many features to which Europeans are unaccustomed, and which therefore often strike them as unpleasing or bizarre; but it must be remembered that use is second nature, and, in considering the many forms which to us verge on the grotesque, we must make allowance for that essential difference between East and West which is further accentuated in purely Eastern architecture by those religious observances and social customs of which, in accordance with our usual method, we shall take due cognisance. These non-historical styles can scarcely be as interesting from an architect's point of view as those of Europe, which have progressed by the successive solution of constructive problems, resolutely met and overcome; for in the East decorative schemes seem generally to have outweighed all other considerations, and in this would appear to lie the main essential differences between Historical and Non-Historical architecture."

These statements, clearly incorrect, have been quoted in order to clear the ground of prejudice and to provide a starting point for a general statement about this architecture. In each Moslem land, this architecture had its roots in the building traditions of pre-Islamic times; it went through historical development from experimental, to developed, to over-developed, forms; it had a distinctive character reflective of local climate, materials, and methods; and from land to land it clearly belonged to one family and one great stream of culture. And, unlike Gothic or Renaissance styles, Islamic architecture is not only a heritage of the past, for it remains alive as new religious structures continue to be erected in the Moslem world.

Islamic architecture is basically (as was Gothic) architecture at the service of religion. Structures erected for Islam included mosques *(masjid, cami, mescit)*, religious schools *(madrasa, medrese)*, convents *(khanaqah, tekke)*, shrines and mausoleums *(mazar, imamzada, gunbad, turbe)*, and —related to mosques and schools—the minaret *(minar, minare)*. In addition to houses, secular structures included palaces, forts, hospitals, caravanserai *(khan, han)*, bazaars, bridges, and fountains. The proportion of surviving secular buildings to religious ones is very small. The rulers of many dynasties erected elegant and spacious palaces. Most were hastily built of impermanent materials. They were deserted by succeeding generations, who erected their own dwellings. Only a few of these vast structures have been uncovered by recent excavations. Bridges and caravanserais, however, have survived throughout the Moslem world.

Nowadays, the monuments of Islamic architecture may be considered from an aesthetic approach or from that of archeologists, who record all the details of individual structures. Preferable is a combination of these approaches—successfully displayed in this present volume. Some words of caution should be sounded in relation to aesthetic judgments. It is a proper approach to analyze such features of construction and design as the relation of solids to voids; the emphasis given to verticality or horizontality; the harmony, or lack of it, between structural forms and applied decoration; the development and change in decorative pattern; color combinations in decoration; the relative relation of color to structure when seen from a distance as compared to close at hand. It is, however, a grievous error to attempt to transfer value judgments and emotional reactions from one culture to another, i.e., to read into Islamic architecture ideas which would have been completely beyond the imagination and desire of the Moslem builders. Unfortunately, this error is fashionable. One author says of the Masjid-i-Shaykh Lutfullah at Isfahan: "The virginal dome . . . there is about it a gentleness which makes it impossible to believe that the great sculptor, as he designed the flowing curves of the dome, was not thinking of a young girl, seeing her breast for a moment in fire-light, glowing with gold among blue shadows, and thereupon he made a dome of gold and blue stone." Elsewhere, however, he remarks " . . . that the domes of mosques—they, too, are the sculptor's memories of bottoms—too full, too round, to be breasts." Moslem society is a very prudish one, and the craftsmen who decided upon the profiles of these domes would have been outraged to hear that they were based on portions of the female anatomy. As far as can be determined, the Moslems read no emotional content into their architecture: their comments were factually descriptive. Of the great tomb of Sultan Sandjar at Merv, the traveler Yakut, who visited it about A.D. 1216, says only: "The blue dome of the tomb could be seen as far as one day's traveling."

Information about the practice of architecture in the Moslem world is very scanty. The specific term for architect, *mi'mar*, is found in inscriptions as early as the 13th century, but the terms that occur over and over again are simply builder, or *banna'*, and *ostad*, or master workman. It is tempting to believe that these builders were members of one among the many craft guilds that flourished throughout the Moslem world and in which technical skills were passed on from generation to generation.

Ibn Khaldun, author of the fascinating *Muqaddimah* (*An Introduction to History*), which was written in the last quarter of the 14th century, wrote briefly about architecture. He stated that architecture was the first and oldest of the sedentary crafts; that building conditions and results varied according to methods, relative skills, climate and wealth; that the quality of the architects depended on the power of the dynasties. Thus, " The monuments of a dynasty are proportionate to its original power. Where it is large and far-flung, with many provinces and subjects, workers are very plentiful and can be brought together from all sides and regions [and] superior social organization and engineering skill [are present]." He also reflected upon the state of architecture in periods of political decline, pointing out that mud brick took the place of stone, that ornamentation was omitted, and that older structures were torn down and their materials reused. His conclusions about the relation of monuments to the original power of a dynasty are very pertinent when applied to the quality and size of the structures erected at the height of the Mughal, Safavid, Timurid, Il-Khanid and Ottoman dynasties, while we can see in Sinan the superior architect whom proper conditions produced.

Manuscripts long since destroyed must have dealt with the craft and science of architecture. Rashid ad-Din, prime minister of the Il-Khanid rulers of Iran at the end of the 13th century and the opening years of the 14th, was a prolific writer. He included among his literary productions a work entitled *Kitabu'l-Ahya wa'l-Athar* (*Book of Animals and Monuments*). No copy of this work has survived, but its table of contents indicates that one chapter concerned the rules to be followed in building houses, structures consecrated to pious purposes, and fortresses, and that another included information on the construction of tombs.

The ritual requirements of the mosque were few in number and were always the same throughout the Moslem world. Each *masjid*, or place of prostration, needed the following: a central area, open or covered, where the faithful could prostrate themselves in prayer; a *mihrab*, or prayer niche, to indicate the direction of Mecca; a *minbar*, or pulpit, adjacent to the *mihrab*; a *minar* from which the people were called to prayer; a basin of water for the ritual washing prior to prayer.

These basic requirements were early supplemented by additional architectural elements, some derived from the pre-Islamic architectural styles of the various countries. A lofty entrance portal led into the central area; if open, this rectangular area was lined with arcades behind which were prayer halls. The area in front of the *mihrab* was treated as a sanctuary, and became a square chamber crowned by a dome. The *iwan*, also *ivan* and *liwan*, a high, rectangular, barrel-vaulted hall completely open at one end, appeared as an element of the entrance portal; it was placed before the sanctuary chamber and became an accent in one or more of the sides of the central area. In Iran a " standard " plan was developed—" standard " in quotation marks, because its builders certainly never thought of it in any such term—for mosque and *madrasa*. An *iwan* portal led into a rectangular open court which had an *iwan* in the center of each of its sides, and the *iwan* opposite the entrance opened into the sanctuary chamber.

In Turkey this standard plan sometimes appeared in the *medrese*, but the plan of the mosque developed quite differently. In the great mosques of the Ottoman period the design was concentrated on the raising of a stately mass high into the air. This mass, preceded by an open forecourt, was basically a dome of great radius supported on a square of four great piers, or an octagon of eight. Within, a vast crowd could assemble under the dome. Architects experimented with the basic form, placing two or four half-domes against the main dome. Taking part in these and other architectural experiments was the renowned architect Sinan (1490-1588), a contemporary of Michelangelo. After one career as a military designer of fortifications, castles and bridges, Sinan became the chief of the corps of architects, and during the rest of his very long life he erected some 360 monuments.

Shrines and tombs abound throughout the Moslem world; many of them are places of pilgrimage, either throughout the year or on special occasions. The so-called tomb towers, octagonal or square structures with an interior dome and an exterior dome or a polyhedral roof, are scattered in their hundreds across the Iranian and Anatolian plateaux. Burial was usually in a basement crypt.

Islamic architecture displays arcuated construction, that is, the use of arched forms. In early structures, arches springing from piers held up flat wooden roofs, but, quite soon, vaults of brick or stone were used to cover all interior areas. Everywhere the builders experimented to see how many types of vaults could be erected over square and rectangular areas, and they produced just as many different types as did the craftsmen of medieval Europe. Domes were highly developed; they stemmed from such prototypes as the rubble masonry domes of Sassanian (pre-Islamic) Iran and the wooden domes of Christian churches in Syria. On the Iranian plateau, very large brick domes were erected without the use of supporting centering, but this was not the case in Anatolia, where the domes of the Ottoman period were put into place over an elaborate system of scaffolding. In Iran, as the domes grew larger and loftier their interior height became out of scale with the plan area of the chamber below, and so a lower dome was inserted below the main one: these double domes (the outer one of slightly bulbous profile) were also found to the east of the Iranian plateau. In Turkey the size of the area under the dome had a considered relationship to the interior height of the dome, and so double domes were not employed. Also, while faience coated the domes of Iran, in Turkey dome exteriors were sheathed with sheets of lead.

Throughout the Moslem world, in all periods except the earliest centuries of Islam, the structural fabric of the monuments is not exposed, but is concealed by decorative revetments. That is to say, a thin ornamental coating was applied to a roughly finished building. Aside from the general interest in the form and function of Islamic architecture, it is the character and quality of its decoration that has a particular appeal today. On the one hand, modern structures in most countries completely lack decoration—even color is sparingly used—and it is at once a change and a challenge to look at monuments on which ornament gives life and vitality to planes and forms. On the other hand, today's taste for abstraction in art is quite in harmony with the nonrepresentational patterns of this ornament.

Throughout the reaches of the Iranian and Anatolian plateaux (Afghanistan, Iran and Turkey), from earliest times, decorative art was primarily nonrepresentational in nature. Patterns were either geometric or based on stylized floral forms. Much has been written (including one entire book) on the allegation that Islam prohibits the portrayal of living creatures. No such prohibition is to be found in the Koran itself, but appears in later traditions of the Prophet Muhammad. Figures of human beings and animals were depicted, notably in miniature paintings, in many periods and places. Living forms do appear in architecture—in sculptured reliefs and in faience panels—but such examples are comparatively rare. A number, however, are to be seen in plates which depict details of the Safavid monuments of Isfahan.

The techniques employed in this applied decoration are clearly and thoroughly described in the main body of this work. Some additional emphasis may be placed on the variety and richness of the forms executed in several media. On the Iranian plateau, three media were used consecutively, with the first overlapping the second in time, and the second carrying over into the period of the third (which actually appeared in tentative experiments with the first): these were baked brick, plaster —sometimes called stucco—and faience.

The bricks were not in the shape now familiar to Europe and to the United States; they were square and quite thin (approximately 25 cm. on a side and 5 cm. thick). Since a brick revetment pattern would not be the full depth of a brick, the bricks were either cut to the required thicknesses or molded into special shapes before firing. Very probably the scaffolding used in the building of the basic fabric of the structure was left in place, so that the team of decorators could work directly from it. Some patterns were laid up directly, much as carpets could be woven without patterns, while others were assembled from precast sections. This precasting of brick patterns was to provide the technique employed in making faience panels. Based on squares and more complex geometrical motifs such as hexagons, octagons and stars, and interlacing combinations of these elements, the patterns displayed great variety. Then, just as the virtuosity of brick patterns seemed to have reached a peak, plaster came on the scene.

Plaster lent itself to even more variety than had brick bonding, since the medium could be used in so many more different ways. Plaster colored to match brick was applied in a thick coating to the core walls of a structure, and, when it had hardened, simulated brick bonding patterns were scratched into the surface. Plaster in relief spread over entire *mihrabs*, appeared in countless inscription bands and even covered large wall surfaces. Some of the very high relief elements were certainly precast, but most of the work was executed by carving the wet and molded plaster with knives and special tools. Wall surfaces were covered with a layer of very hard white plaster with decorative designs painted in colors; many of the designs were done through the use of stencils. In this type of decoration, design elements were grouped together, and very large areas of plain white plaster were left unornamented, whereas in the plasterwork in relief all areas were colored.

Faience, in the form of enameled tiles, took over from plaster. Small segments of glazed tile had provided sparse accents of color to the brick bonding patterns. Then color began to spread over the structure, until it reached a fantastic degree of brilliance and impact in the Timurid period. Faience mosaic covered entire surfaces of monuments. In this technique the craftsmen began with square, brick-sized tiles, coated with a fired color glaze in one of a number of colors. Light blue and an intense dark blue were the predominant hues. Following a full-scale pattern drawn either on paper or on a prepared bed of white plaster, the craftsmen hacked away at the tiles with tiny hatchets to produce small pieces of tile which, when laid glazed side down on the pattern of a panel, gradually filled it up. Then the backs of the pieces were coated with plaster, and, when this had hardened, each panel was installed on the surface of the structure. This technique was very time-consuming and hence very costly. It did produce an extraordinary effect: each fragment of tile was set in the plaster bed at a slight angle to the others, so that the light falling across a completed surface created a remarkable sparkle and contrast.

Within the Safavid period the technique of faience mosaic gave way to the less expensive technique of *haft rangi* (seven colors), described briefly in the text. There the standard square tiles were decorated with a small segment of a larger design; the details of the design were painted with one of seven different coloring materials, and the tiles were then given a single firing in the furnaces. At its best, *haft rangi* work is hard to distinguish from faience mosaic, but most of this work reflects a marked decline in craftmanship and devotion to design.

Turkey went through a different phase in the decorative development of its architecture. Faience mosaic came into use at least as early as in Iran, and reached a crescendo at Bursa. *Haft rangi* tiles (to transfer this Persian term) were used throughout the Ottoman period. In building, however, the Turkish genius lay in the use of dressed and carved stone. Greater Anatolia was a stone-carving center as early as the time of the Greeks and the Achaemenids, and this tradition carried on over the succeeding centuries. For example, the lovely stone churches of Armenia clearly influenced the forms and carving of the Moslem tomb towers.

In the Moslem world, as in the lands of the West, architecture had the status of a major art, while sculpture did not attain this rank because of the prohibition previously discussed. Two other crafts, which had no such prestige in the Western world, achieved the rank of major arts in Islam. These were calligraphy and carpet-weaving, including, of course, carpet design. Although documentary material is scanty, there was in both Turkey and Iran a clear relationship between these crafts and architecture. One of the greatest calligraphers of Safavid times, whose talent was devoted primarily to manuscripts, designed the inscriptions of the Masjid-i-Shaykh Lutfullah, while many of the faience mosaic panels of the monuments at Isfahan are reminiscent of the carpets woven at that same time. These conclusions hold true for Turkey as well, although Turkish carpets display different designs from Iranian ones, show a different palette of preferred colors and have a less close relationship to architectural ornament.

The amazing number of inscriptions preserved on the monuments of Iran and Turkey, and the different types of scripts employed, bear witness to the high state of development of calligraphy. Such inscriptions were almost without exception in Arabic, and were intelligible to a mere handful of religious scholars. Throughout the Seljuk period, an archaic form dating from the first centuries of Islam, called Kufic, was favored: in this script the letters are blocky and crowded together, as may be noticed on the inscriptions of the tombs at Kharraqan. Later, distinctive forms such as Naskhi and Thulth came into use, but regardless of the name of the script the concern of the calligrapher was in creating a harmony with the surfaces of the structure. Thus one script might emphasize bold vertical strokes, another could stress horizontal movement, a third might show a flowing movement with spaced accents, and still another would display a second line of script set within the vertical strokes of the lower line. These and other variations should be sought in the plates which follow, as should those forms that are so completely stylized as to appear at first glance to be pure geometric ornament. Moslem architecture, with its integration of other arts and crafts into architecture—and given the major role of religious edifices in Islamic society—should be viewed as a comprehensive reflection of a highly developed and enduring faith and culture.

DONALD N. WILBER

Princeton, New Jersey

AFGHANISTAN AND IRAN

Afghanistan and Iran have long and complex artistic traditions.

Craftsmen of Luristan (mid-second millenium B.C.), Archaemenians, Parthians, Gandaharans, and Sassanians all contributed to the heritage of the Islamic period. From antiquity Afghanistan and Iran have been strategically located on major commercial and military routes. The old Silk Road from China crossed the area, and Alexander the Great traversed these lands leaving Greek colonies in his wake. Arabic influence was exercised by the architectural requirements and stylistic background of the dominant religion of Mohammed. After the devastating Mongol invasions (13th to 15th centuries), periods of prosperity and fruitful artistic activity ensued. New ideas from Central Asia and the Far East were absorbed into the cultural tradition. The architecture that evolved in Afghanistan and Iran was influenced by this inheritance, by climatic factors, and available building materials.

A stark desert environment stimulated a desire for intricate patterns and brilliant color. The palaces of Persepolis had elaborately carved walls; Sassanian rock-cut reliefs were marvels of complex design. The typical, completely enclosed Arab mosque was unsuited to the milder climate of Afghanistan and Iran, where open courtyards were customary. Mosque plans which emerged here provided for an arcaded court; usually only the sanctuary chamber was covered by a dome. In domestic architecture, high spacious porches *(talars)*—appropriate to the climate—were built. With slender wooden columns and relatively massive roofs, these *talars* characterized palace architecture for many centuries.

In the Islamic period stone was rarely used, but brick—which was readily available—was employed in many ways to create patterned surfaces.

Afghanistan and Iran were significant contributors to the artistic development of many lands. Timur took Iranian craftsmen to Samarkand and Bukhara for the construction and decoration of his monuments. Babur, the founder of the Moghul dynasty in India, brought to the sub-continent the artistic traditions of Afghanistan. In the 16th and 17th centuries, Iranian designers were influential in India; and—as will be seen in the second section of this volume—Iran has exerted strong stylistic influences on Turkey.

CHAPTER I # Pre-Seljuk
and
Seljuk
Periods

(A.D. 1037-1194; A.H. 428-591)

The most striking characteristic of early Islamic
architecture in Iran is the use of brick, for both
structure and decoration. This era is sometimes
referred to as the " naked brick " period. Many
new types of brick ornamentation were employed;
they ranged from bold patterns for large walls
to minute, intricate work for panels. Color
appeared in a few interior frescoes and occasionally
in tiles which were used to accent a façade, but
it was only in Maragha—at the close of the
epoch—that it assumed a major decorative role.

GURGAN. Gunbad-i-Kabus

The Gunbad-i-Kabus (tomb tower of Kabus) in Gurgan bears the inscribed date A.H. 397 (A.D. 1006-7). The building has a diameter of 56 feet (17.08 m.) at the foundation course and a height of 167 feet (51 m.) from the plinth to the top of the roof. The tower goes down for about 35 feet (10.75 m.) more beneath an artificial hillock, which would make the original height above ground approximately 200 feet (61 m.). The bricks are square and measure about 8¼ inches (20.8 cm.) by nearly two inches (4.7 cm.) thick. They are hard fired and are so fine in composition that they ring when struck. Specially shaped bricks were used on the roof. [1]

This mausoleum was built for Kabus ibn Washmgir, ruler of Gurgan from 976 to about 1012 (A.H. 365 to about 403). According to legend, Kabus' coffin was suspended high in the building so that the rays of the sun shining through a small window could greet him daily.

Wake! For the Sun behind yon Eastern height
Has chased the Session of the Stars from Night;
And, to the field of Heav'n ascending, strikes
The Sultan's Turret with a Shaft of Light.

Omar Khayyam, *Rubaiyat* [2]

SANGBAST. Tomb

The tomb at Sangbast (A.D. 997-1028; A.H. 387-419) is generally believed to have been built by the Governor of Tus, Arslan Jadhib. Eric Schroeder points out in his analysis of the construction of this building that " a brick ring twenty-five courses deep acts as abutment or weight on the haunch and perhaps this is the oldest Persian work embodying the knowledge that a dome is stronger if lighter at the crown."[1] A chevron pattern is found on the inside of the dome, and the walls are decorated with a design in incised plaster.

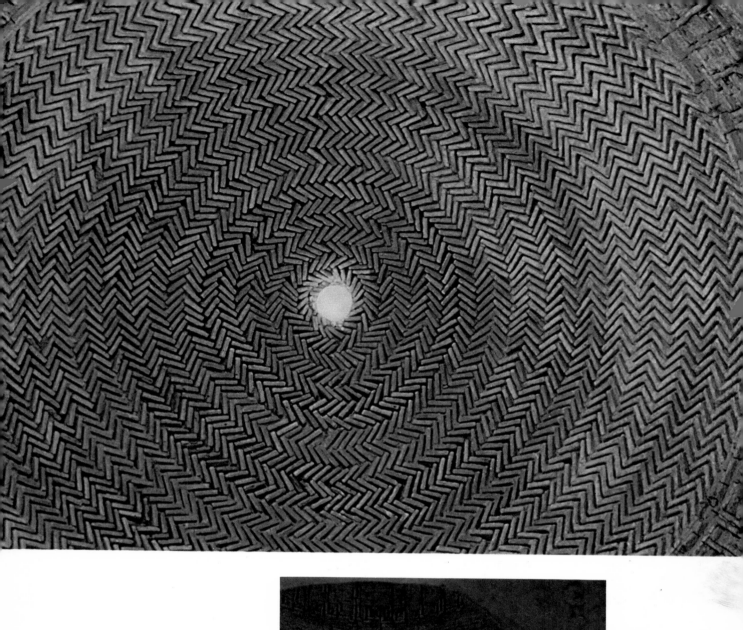

DEMAVAND. Tomb tower

This Seljuk tomb tower, situated on a hill above
and to the east of the village of Demavand,
was probably erected early in the third quarter of
the 11th century (5th century A.H.). The brick
walls of the octagonal structure are faced with a
decorative brick revetment. The external
height of the tower, from the stone foundation
to the top of the octagonal dome, is 32 feet
(9.89 m.). The diameter on the inside, at
floor level, is about 16 feet (4.85 m.).

PLATE 5

DEMAVAND. Tomb tower

Detail of lower left-hand panel in Plate 4.

PLATE 6

DEMAVAND. Tomb tower

A flush, diaper bond is used for the chevron
pattern of these panels from the northeast wall of
the Seljuk tomb tower near Demavand.

DEMAVAND. Seljuk tomb tower

The brickwork on the engaged columns, with its
wide interstices and recessed bonding, increases the
textural quality of the outside of this tomb.
The deep mortar bed is achieved by a technique
known as finger-impressed jointing.

PLATE 8

DEMAVAND. Seljuk tomb tower

In the top panel over the reconstructed entrance,
a design of eight-pointed stars forms an alternate
cruciform pattern. The lower panels which
flank the doorway show positive and negative
versions of one pattern.

ISFAHAN. Masjid-i-Jami

These columns and vaults are in the northeast
section of the Masjid-i-Jami, Isfahan.
Although the hall shown here was built during
the Muzaffarid period (A.D. 1340-90; A.H. 741-92),
it is in the Seljuk naked brick style.

Isfahan was described in 1052 (A.H. 444) by
the traveler Nasir-i-Khusrau:

It is a town situated on a plain; it has an agreeable
climate, and wherever one sinks a well to a depth
of ten gaz (approximately 36 feet or 11 m.) very
cold and good water flows out. The city has a strong and
high wall, with gates and fortifications, and on all
the walls there are battlements. Inside there are streams
of running water and fine and lofty buildings;
in the center of the city is the great and magnificent
Masjid-i-Jami. They say that the walls of the city
are three-and-a-half farsangs (slightly over twelve miles,
or twenty kilometers) in length. The interior of the city
is uniformly prosperous in appearance, and I did not see
a single building in ruins. I noticed many bazaars,
and in one of these, which was that of the money changers,
there were two hundred men of this profession.
Each bazaar has its wall and its gate, as has every
quarter and street. There are clean and well-kept
caravanserais. The caravan of which we formed part had
brought thirteen hundred kharvars of goods (about
nine thousand camel-loads). When we entered the city
no one noticed our arrival; there was so much room
that there was no difficulty in obtaining lodging
and food. I have never seen, in any place where Persian
is spoken, a finer, larger and more prosperous city
than Isfahan.[1]

PLATE 10

ISFAHAN. Masjid-i-Jami

The Gunbad-i-Khark (also known as the
northeast dome chamber), in the Masjid-i-Jami
at Isfahan, was erected during the reign of
Malik Shah and under the patronage of his vizier
Nizam al-Mulk. This structure, which is
inscribed with the date A.H. 481 (A.D. 1088), is
65 feet 6 inches (20 m.) high; the inner
diameter of the dome measures 32 $^4/_5$ feet (10 m.).
Despite severe earthquakes this single-dome chamber
has stood intact for almost nine hundred years.
Dr. Arthur Upham Pope refers to it as being
both structurally and aesthetically " one of the
most remarkable buildings in Islam." [2] The chamber
is built entirely of brick, and the uniformity of
material emphasizes the singleness of purpose
with which the square base rises, through
the columns and arches and squinches, until
it merges with the superb dome. Attention is
focused on the structural elements and on the
resolution of the problems they pose, and the result
is an architectural harmony achieved through the
stringent terms of engineering.

ISFAHAN. Masjid-i-Jami

The collar of the cupola forms a firm base for the
dome of the Gunbad-i-Khark, yet the tall
Kufic inscription is conceived so as to continue the
strong vertical character of the lower chamber.
Like the ultimate chord in a symphony, the
dome is the final solution of the structural
drama. Here sophisticated design challenges
interpretation. Vertical motion ceases; the
area of contemplation has been reached.
The geometric patterns in the dome are composed
of a series of triangles which evolve into two
five-pointed stars.

ISFAHAN. Masjid-i-Jami

The library vaults of the Masjid-i-Jami
were probably built between 1121 and 1175
(A.H. 515-571) in Seljuk times.[3] Documents survive,
which record the destruction of the greater
part of the mosque in 1121-22 (A.H. 515) by
a fire which left only the domed sanctuary of
Nizam al-Mulk and the northeast dome chamber
intact. Reconstruction was begun immediately.
It was at this time that the plan of the Masjid-i-Jami
was changed from that of a kiosk mosque,
which has individual, isolated buildings, to that
of a *madrasa* mosque with four *iwans* centered
on each side of a rectangular arcaded court
(Plate 83). [4]

The library vaults are located southeast of the
sanctuary *iwan*. Plate 12 shows vault 47.
Plate 13 shows vault 60 in the foreground. Behind
it, on the right, is vault 61; on the left is vault 47.
(Vault numbers are from the Herzfeld plan.)[5]
The small units of brick allow great flexibility
in design. An important attribute of brick as a
medium is that it permits variety within a
unified whole. With it the artist could create
harmonious areas of vast proportions (such
as these halls in the Masjid-i-Jami), each segment
of which still maintained its particular individuality.

PLATE **14**

ISFAHAN. Masjid-i-Jami

This view of library vault 60 (Herzfeld plan)
shows a skillful use of ribs. Recent repairs made
in this hall necessitated the removal of
the intervening vault sections, and it was
discovered that these ribs are self-sustaining—the
material between them (as in Gothic vaulting)
playing no part in their support.

پ و ۴۱

ISFAHAN. Masjid-i-Jami

Plate 15 shows a typical closed vault which gets its ornamentation from the pattern of its brick lay. Color other than white is introduced only in the form of variations in the tones of the brick.

Plate 16 is a view of vault 62 (Herzfeld plan).

PLATE 17

KHARRAQAN. Tomb towers

These two Seljuk brick tomb towers, located near
Hisar-i-Armani in the Kharraqan region of
western Iran, were discovered in 1963, by
William Miller. They were first described by
David Stronach. On the right, or eastern, side we
see the earlier building, dated A.H. 460
(A.D. 1067-68); the later mausoleum, on the left,
is dated A.H. 486 (A.D. 1093). Both dates are
inscribed. In all probability the tombs were the
work of one architect, a Persian of local origin called
Muhammad b. Makki al Zanjani on one tomb
and Abu'l Ali b. Makki al Zanjani on the other.
The octagonal towers stand slightly more
than 40 feet (13 m.) above ground and have a
diameter of 34 feet (10.4 m.). As at Demavand, the
brick core of the structures is adorned with a
decorative brick revetment. For additional
embellishment, the engaged arches of the
later Kharraqan tower are divided into two major
panels with a row of three small arches separating
them. Together the two tombs display some
seventy different brick designs. The towers have
double domes—the earliest examples as
yet found in Iran—and enclosed spiral staircases.

PLATE 18

KHARRAQAN. Tomb tower

Around the upper part of the arch in this detail
from the later Kharraqan tomb tower is a simple
border composed of single bricks alternating
with two
the slende
rounded
the morta
structural
but more
later, by s
task. The
during con
revetment.

KHARRAQAN. Tomb tower

Plate 19 shows the upper half of an arch panel on the later Kharraqan tomb tower. The pattern—which at a later date was repeated in mosaic tile—has remarkable mobility and seems to change from varying viewpoint or in different lights.

Plate 20 is a panel over the entrance to the earlier tomb. Whole and half-size bricks are used in an asymmetrical composition of opposing diagonals.

PLATE **21**

KHARRAQAN. Tomb tower

The panel detail shown here is from the earlier
Kharraqan tomb. Iranian builders used brick in
a variety of sizes, from the large square bricks
(8¼ inches in the Gunbad-i-Kabus) to very small
kinds fired in special molds. The bricks
were frequently cut into the desired shapes while
wet, with a sharp knife or wire. This was the
technique employed at Kharraqan.
Another variation was achieved through changing
the mortar bed. Not only did the builders vary
the spacing between bricks; they also treated
the mortar in different ways—having it flush
with the bricks in some areas and deeply recessed in
others.

KHARRAQAN. Tomb tower

The detail opposite is from the later Kharraqan tomb tower. The design on the center niche seems, at first glance, very free. As can be seen from Figure A, it is actually a part of a formal geometric design. The skillful way in which the artist framed the motif, however, gives no more than a hint of the repeated pattern.

Their rich covering of brick decoration gives these towers (and the Demavand tomb in Plates 4-8) a textural, tweed-like quality.

Figure A. Pattern of design fragment in center niche, Plate 22.

KHARRAQAN. Tomb tower

The details opposite are from the earlier
Kharraqan tomb tower. Plate 23 shows a frieze
on the southwest elevation. The segments
which connect the three wheels in this design are
the hubs of other wheels which are cut off
by the border of the frieze. Wheels and spokes,
punctuated by the brick dot which is the axle, seem
to revolve together endlessly.

Part of the west elevation is seen in Plate 24.

*Note: The wheel design on the endpapers is derived
from Plate 23.*

KHARRAQAN. Tomb tower

Inside the arch, in this detail from the later Kharraqan tomb tower, is a pattern composed of pairs of sinuous lines which cross one another at various angles. Here and there the intersecting lines form a hexagon. Inside this is another hexagon, of raised brick, with a ring of mortar and a single brick at its center.

Iranian friezes are often more static than the wall designs, and provide areas of repose. This decorative band is marked by deep shadows, so that the raised and recessed areas of the pattern are equal in value. The scheme appears to derive from a stylized branch. In Figure B the three-pronged motifs interpenetrate to form a repeating pattern.

Figure B. Detail of pattern of frieze, Plate 25.

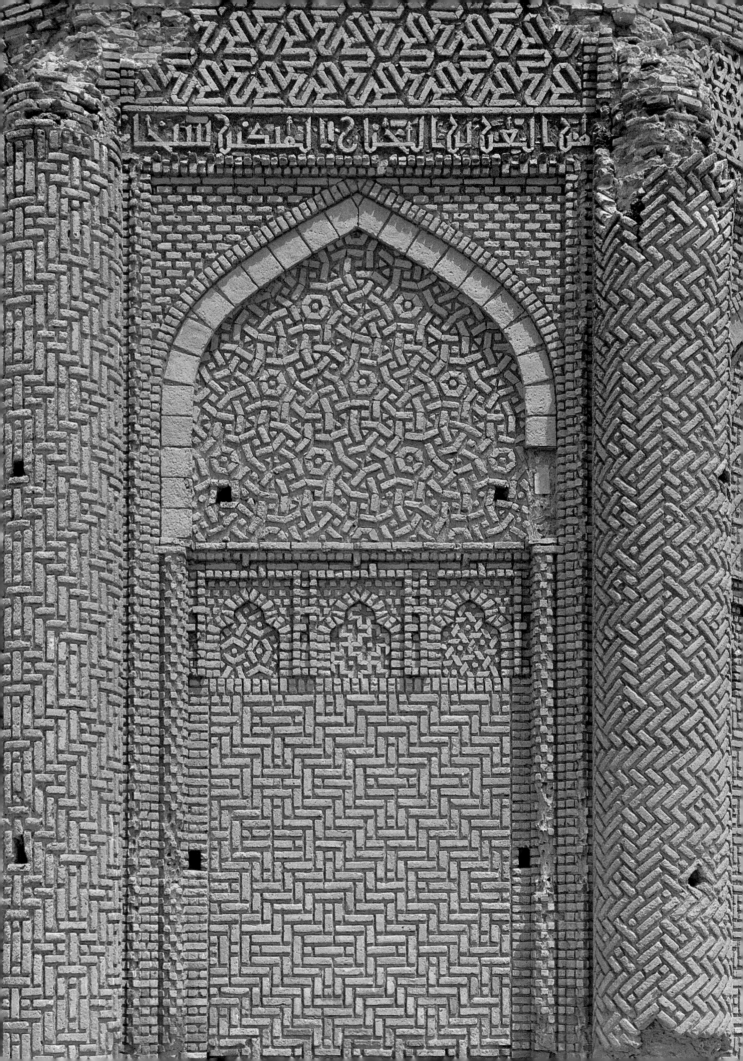

KHARRAQAN. Tomb tower

The panel shown opposite, from the later
Kharraqan tower, is the panel to the right (east) of
that in Plate 25. The staccato rhythm of the
small cut bricks in the moldings gives a sharp
outline to the panel. This is further accentuated by
the use of a similar technique on the slender
applied columns. Often, intricate patterns such as
those in the niches were set up in wooden frames, as
depicted in Figure C. Sometimes bricks
were laid on more than one plane. Deeply
recessed mortar was achieved through the insertion
of wood fillers. After the mortar had set, the
frame would be removed and the finished
panel attached to the wall as a unit.

*Figure C. Wooden frame used for setting up a wall
decoration. (After Jacobstahl.)*[1]

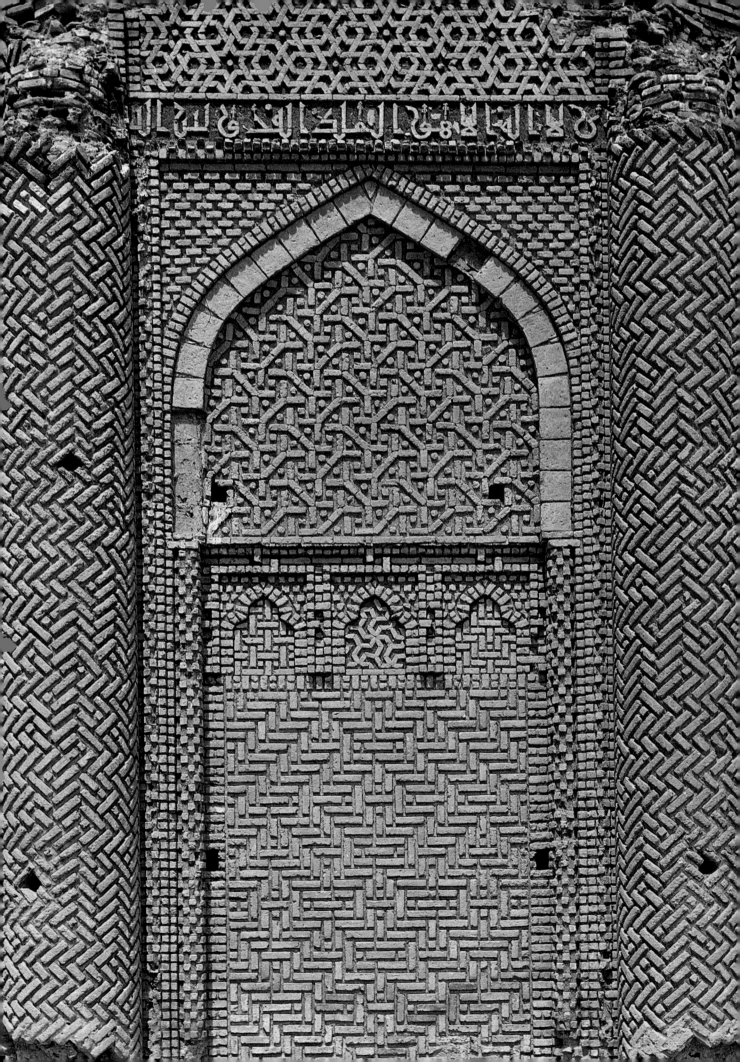

PLATE 27

NAYIN. Masjid-i-Jami

In the court of the Masjid-i-Jami at Nayin
(built *circa* 960 [A.H. 350]) is a brick *iwan*
of great simplicity and dignity of conception. The
pattern of the diminutive balustrade and the
spiral brickwork on the half-columns are
heightened by the sunlight and enliven the façade.
The high relief of the brickwork on the
cornice hints at power and reserve, qualities
suggested also by other features of this building.
(The lower blocking walls and the buttresses seen
here are modern.)

This is a very early Iranian mosque, and
its large columned hall still shows the strong
influence of the Arab style. The *mihrab* and *minbar*
are decorated with magnificent stucco work. As
these features have been illustrated fairly
often, they have not been included here.[1]

PLATE **28**

TABAS. Caravanserai

The courtyard of the caravanserai at Tabas is shown
here. Situated near the center of the
Great Salt Desert, Tabas blisters in summer under
a merciless sun; this makes shade a necessity
and enhances the aesthetic appeal of
shadow. The lower cornice molding of rounded
bricks, which protrudes only slightly from the flat
surface, achieves a distinctive effect. Although
the caravanserai was erected in the early
20th century (A.H. 1327 or 1337), this style of
brick building has been traditional for hundreds
of years.

PLATE **29**

TABAS. Caravanserai

Strong lines of raised brick lead into the modeled
plaster of the dome in the caravanserai.

MARAGHA. Gunbad-i-Surkh

Gunbad-i-Surkh, in Maragha is about 27½ feet
(8.44 m.) high measured from the outside. It was
once covered by an eight-sided pyramidal roof.
The builder of this square tomb tower was
Bakr Muhammad. Erected in 1147-48 (A.H. 542),
the structure shows an early use of colored tile
with brick. The novel decoration around
the entrance is in several simple patterns which
closely imitate brick designs (Plate 19). The
contrast in texture of gleaming tile against the mat
finish of brick produced some of the finest
effects in Iranian architecture. In the
course of the next four centuries enameled brick
was combined with natural brick and stucco
in varying proportions. Ultimately, panels
and even entire mosques were designed in
polychrome tile—a technique which resulted in an
effect of overwhelming brilliance.

PLATE 32

MARAGHA. Gunbad-i-Surkh

This view of the south and east walls of the
Gunbad-i-Surkh shows how the designer
transformed the square base into an
octagonal support for the flat interior dome. Above
the square stone masonry base the corners
appear cut off at a 45 degree angle to the main
brick façades. Engaged columns add strength and
aesthetic interest to the design.

MARAGHA. Gunbad-i-Surkh

This detail is from the east wall of the
Gunbad-i-Surkh. The form of the engaged corner
column is stressed by a deep shadow which
terminates within the stone cap. Half-size and full-
size bricks, laid vertically in an alternating
pattern form the cornice.[1]

PLATE 34

MARAGHA. Gunbad-i-Kabud

The Gunbad-i-Kabud, also at Maragha, is an octagonal tomb tower with a pyramidal roof, the upper part of which has been destroyed. Built in 1196-97 (A.H. 593), this tomb was modeled on that of Muminah Khatun at Nakhichevan.[2] Virtuosity is displayed in the complex brick patterns which are intermingled with glazed tiles. All the decorative materials on the facing are minute and give the effect of a glistening net enmeshing the tower. This view shows the west and northwest sides, including the entrance.

MARAGHA. Gunbad-i-Kabud

This detail from the west wall of the
Gunbad-i-Kabud shows a network of dressed
brick patterns which is composed chiefly of
pentagons and hexagons.

PLATE **36**

MARAGHA. Gunbad-i-Kabud

This view of the west side of the Gunbad-i-Kabud shows the glazed tile inscription on the frieze. Above it is a stalactite cornice.

CHAPTER II

Il-Khanid Period

(A.D. 1256-*circa* 1340; A.H. 654-*circa* 741)

The descendants of Genghis Khan's grandson Hulagu, who were known as the Il-Khans, ruled over a large section of Iran and Iraq for about a hundred years. During this period there was a marked increase in the use of color for decorative effects in architecture. Buildings became more monumental, and verticality was stressed increasingly. Mongol designers frequently used a single dome rather than a double one, which meant that the lofty exterior was repeated in a high interior.

After the first wave of conquest, the Mongol rulers of Iran became deeply interested in the beautification and cultural development of the country. A letter written at the end of the 14th century by the vizier and historian Rashid ad-Din illustrates the scope of their humanistic endeavors. The historian is writing to his son and is reporting on the progress of an educational center that he has founded in Tabriz:

Therefore we have sent, with the utmost celerity, letters and couriers to the scholars of the time and learned of the epoch, saying, "Turn the bridle of your setting out toward us; for we would, henceforth, provide means for you to spread knowledge in peace of mind." Now crowds of scholars and men of science arrive continually and we do our best to keep them free of cares ... The Rab,-i-Rashidi, for the establishment and construction of which we had already made plans and preparations at the time of your departure, is now complete. In it we have built twenty four caravanserais, fifteen hundred ... shops and thirty thousand charming houses. Baths, pleasant gardens, store [houses], mills, factories for cloth weaving and paper making, a dye house and a mint have also been constructed.

People from every city and country have been removed to the said foundation ... Among them are two hundred reciters of the Qur'an . . . and we have given dwellings to four hundred other scholars, theologians, jurists and traditionalists, in the street which is named the "Street of the Scholars"; daily payments, pensions, yearly clothing allowances, soap money and sweet money have been granted for them all.[1]

Figure D. View of Tabriz in the 17th century, from Chardin.

Apart from a brief interlude at Sultaniya during the reigns of Oljeitu and Abu Said, the Il-Khanid capital was at Tabriz. Trade routes moved northward, away from Baghdad, and Tabriz became the major commercial center of the empire. In 1320 there was a Venetian settlement in the city, and in 1341 the Genoese had a factory there, which was supervised by a consul with a council of twenty-four merchants. In 1340 Mustawfi commented on the magnificent buildings of the metropolis. He noted that there were over nine hundred underground waterways for the irrigation of the extensive gardens and orchards.

PLATE 37

TABRIZ. Masjid-i-Ali Shah

The massive walls shown here are on the
Masjid-i-Ali Shah (the Arg), in Tabriz
(A.D. 1313-22; A.H. 712-22). The side walls, which
are built of fired brick, are 34 feet (10.4 m.)
thick. Foundation measurements indicate that
the distance between the portal and the
mihrab was over 215 feet (65.55 m.).
This mosque was constructed under the patronage
of, and may have been designed by, Taj ad-Din
Ali Shah, a jewel merchant who rose to
become vizier in the reigns of emperors Oljeitu
and Abu Said. Like his contemporary, Rashid
ad-Din, Taj ad-Din Ali Shah was a lavish
patron of the arts.[1] It was his intention that this
building should surpass all other monuments in
magnificence, including Ctesiphon. Ibn Battuta,
writing between 1330 and 1340, described
the mosque as having a forecourt paved with
marble and walls decorated with faience.
The arches of the surrounding portico were adorned
with gold. An Italian merchant, visiting in
1514, added that the columns in the portico were
of a marble " so fine and so transparent
that they resemble fine crystal." [2]

Figure E. Restored plan of the Masjid-i-Ali Shah.

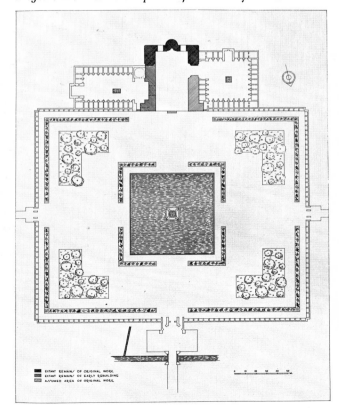

SULTANIYA

Figure F. View of Sultaniya in the 17th century, from Chardin.

In 1304 (A.H. 703) Sultaniya was selected by the ruler Oljeitu as the site for his capital, and within a few years he had erected a magnificent city. Climate and geography, however, doomed Sultaniya to extinction, and today only the mausoleum of Oljeitu looms above the mud dwellings—ghost of a glorious whim. The Spanish ambassador, Clavijo, bound on a mission to Timur in Samarkand, visited Sultaniya in 1404. Although this was almost a hundred years after the death of Oljeitu, the Spaniard's account recaptures some of the city's earlier splendor:

On Thursday the 26th of June we finally arrived at the great city of Sultaniyah. It is a very populous city, but not so great as Tabriz; though it is a more important center of exchange for merchants and their goods. In June, July, and August each year large caravans arrive with foods from India, Syria, Turkey, and all parts of the empire—spices, silks, cottons, pearls, rubies, and all manner of merchandise are brought to the Summer fairs. The city of Sultaniyah lies in a plain, and the town is intersected by many water conduits. We saw fine streets and squares where much merchandise was exposed for sale: while in all quarters hostels are to be met with, very conveniently disposed for the accommodation of the merchants who come to the city. Standing some distance outside the city is an immense [mosque and] palace of many apartments that was built in past times by a certain great lord, whose body was later buried here in a magnificent tomb.

Prince Miran Shah, the son of Timur, awaited our coming. We were brought to him at one of his palaces which stands in a fine orchard and there were many attendants-in-waiting present. He received us in a tent where his abode was that day established, and very graciously enquired of us as to the health of the King of Spain, our master. Afterwards when the time came for us to take our leave, the attendants brought in robes made of gold brocade in which they dressed each of us ambassadors, and we then returned to our lodgings.[1]

PLATE 38

SULTANIYA. Mausoleum of Oljeitu Khudabanda

The mausoleum of Oljeitu Khudabanda was
built in Sultaniya in 1304-13 (A.H. 703-13). The
basic structure is an octagon about 80 feet
(24.5 m.) across on the inside. At the base the walls
are almost 23 feet (7 m.) thick, giving a total
width of approximately 126 feet (39 m.). The
interior height of the single dome is about 175 feet
(about 53 m.). André Godard has described
this monument as " . . . the skillful,
confident work of a great builder, a consummate
technician who was at the same time an artist.
Here is a dome with a span of 80 feet built solely of
bricks, without any buttresses, pinnacles,
or shoulders of any kind, which stands simply by
virtue of a perfectly conceived and constructed
profile."[2]

PLATE **39**

SULTANIYA. Mausoleum of Oljeitu

The detail seen here is from the cornice on the east
side of the Oljeitu mausoleum at Sultaniya.
This is the earliest major monument in Iran in
which color has been used for massive effects. The
dome was covered with tiles of turquoise,
while the façade was decorated in shades of deep
blue. Stalactites adorn the cornice and increase the
play of light and shadow. Through the arch
the elaborate patterns on the walls
of the upper galleries can be seen.

The construction of a splendid capital in
little more than a decade appears an incredible
achievement. At this time, however, artisans were
protected and greatly valued by the Eastern
warlords. The capture of a town often meant the
massacre of the inhabitants—with the exception of
the craftsmen. These artisans were
promptly conscripted and sent to work in the
conqueror's cities. A vast number of men
labored on the monuments of Sultaniya.

As late as the Safavid period, the skill of
its artisans was still regarded as an
inestimable wealth of a kingdom. At that time
some trades paid a tax into the royal treasury, but
craftsmen, especially in the building field,
owed their tribute in labor. The chief architect
of a monument was not only highly respected but
was also well remunerated, receiving as salary up to
twenty per cent of the assessed value of the work.

PLATE 40

SULTANIYA. Mausoleum of Oljeitu

The upper galleries of the mausoleum of Oljeitu
present vistas of painted and carved stucco
designs which glow in shades of red.[3] The brick
walls were covered with a smooth surface
of hard plaster into which the patterns were
cut to a depth of about three-eighths of an inch
(about a centimeter) and then painted
with distemper. It is extremely likely that
decorative details from illuminated manuscripts were
used in the ornamentation of buildings. A Koran
in the National Assembly Library, Cairo, which was
written in Hamadan for Oljeitu, contains patterns
almost identical with the stucco decoration
in the galleries shown here.[4]

PLATE **41**

SULTANIYA. Mausoleum of Oljeitu

This vault is in the upper galleries of the
mausoleum of Oljeitu. These galleries encircle the
building at the third story level but do not
communicate with the interior.

PLATE **42**

SULTANIYA. **Mausoleum of Oljeitu**

Star motifs, as in this vault in the upper galleries
of the Oljeitu mausoleum, occur frequently and
in a variety of forms. This particular
example has a modeled surface which is pleasingly
adapted to the vault area.

SULTANIYA. **Mausoleum of Oljeitu**

PLATE 43

SULTANIYA. Mausoleum of Oljeitu

This detail from the upper galleries of the
Oljeitu mausoleum shows decoration in painted
carved plaster. Carved stucco insets simulate brick
and plugs. Bands of twining foliage and an
interlaced geometric design define the panels and
accent the structural forms.

PLATE 44

SULTANIYA. Mausoleum of Oljeitu

From the outside the height of the dome of
the Oljeitu mausoleum is partially concealed by
the bulk of the octagon. From inside, however,
where the height at the center of the dome is 175 feet,
the silent majesty of space is overwhelming.
Fragments of the original decoration of
glazed tile and stucco can be seen on the arch
leading to the sanctuary.

SULTANIYA. Mausoleum of Oljeitu

Details of the original glazed tile and fine, carved
stucco in the main chamber evoke speculation
as to why blue was so much preferred by the early
Iranian artists. Did a superstitious
belief in the power of blue as protection
against the evil eye have any significance? Many
beads and amulets were—and still are—in that
color for magic reasons. Might the selection
have been determined by some association
with the sky and the heavens? Or did it
stem from something more mundane, such as the
availability of copper compound with which to
make the glaze?[5]

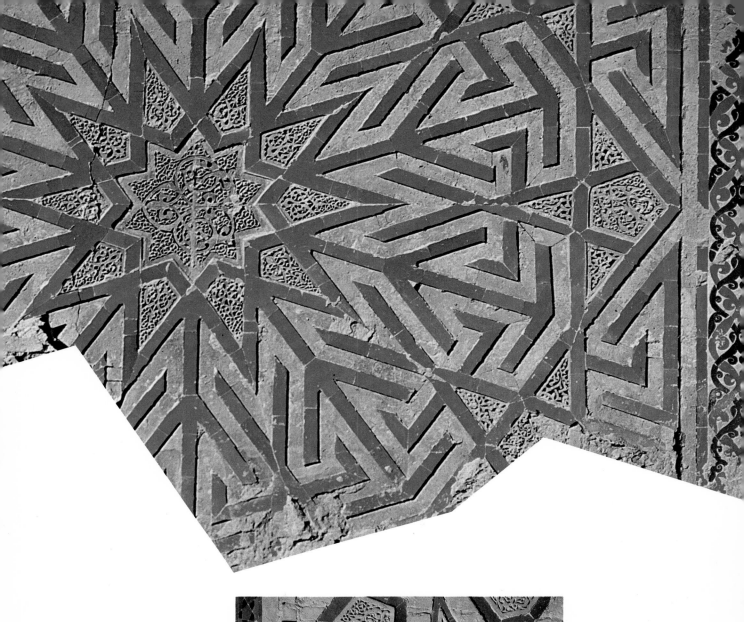

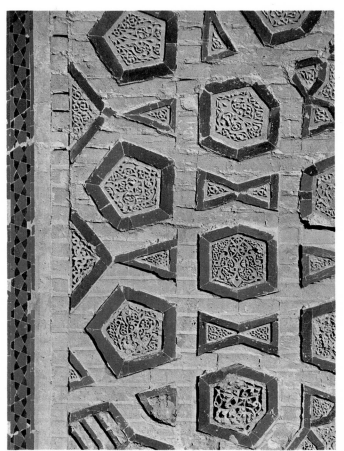

PLATE **47**

SULTANIYA. Mausoleum of Chelebi Oglu

The mausoleum of Chelebi Oglu (A.D. 1310;
A.H. 710) [1] is the only other building remaining
from the 14th century in Sultaniya. It is
an octagonal structure of brick, built on a stone
foundation and having a domed roof. Symmetrical
designs in brick decorate the lower part
of the walls. The golden evening light points up
the patterning of the brick end plugs. This
patterning was a favored method, in
the 14th century, of enlivening a masonry
surface. The plugs were made of hard plaster,
which was either carved with a knife while still soft
or stamped out with wooden blocks. Shaped
bricks (made in specially formed molds and then
fired) surround the deeply recessed
panel. The molding steps up and inward in
three rows—a flush, then a curved, and finally a
diagonal course.

PLATE **48**

BISTAM. Sanctuary of Bayazid Bistami

This detail is from a panel on the southwest side
of the entrance portal to the sanctuary of
Bayazid Bistami at Bistam (A.D. 1313; A.H. 713).
Two overall patterns in glazed tile adorn
the wall. The linear character of the
upper pattern contrasts with the curving forms
in the lower section. Although the upper
panel is a composition which repeats the
name " Ali, " the basic element of both designs is
the swastika.

In Iran, religious centers often arose in regions
associated with a saint. Such shrines included
the tomb of the saint and sometimes a
mosque, a *madrasa* and, occasionally, a monastery
(khanaqah). Muhammad ibn al-Husayn ibn Talib
of Damghan was the architect of this sanctuary.

BISTAM. Masjid-i-Jami

The cloister of the Masjid-i-Jami at Bistam
was built in 1302 (A.H. 702), probably at the
command of Ghazan Khan, as the inscription reads,
" by the order of the Great Amir."
The architect was Muhammad ibn al-Husayn ibn
Talib of Damghan, in collaboration with his
brother Hajji.

Stucco patterns transform the walls of the
small cloister into a lacelike filigree.
Between the two graceful friezes with their
inscriptions, a geometric fretwork restrains the
exuberant design and lends texture to the wall. This
pattern has a six-petaled flower in the center
of a hexagon. This six-sided figure is
surrounded by another hexagon. As in the wheel
design at Kharraqan (Plate 23) the forms
interlock to create a repeated motif.

PLATE **50**

LINJAN. Pir-i-Bakran

The panel shown here is in the mausoleum of
Pir-i-Bakran, built in 1303 (A.H. 703) at Linjan.
Incised plaster designs were used frequently by
the Il-Khanids and often made up individual
plaques on walls. The plaque opposite
consists of a Kufic inscription which is a salutation
to the twelve imams. Pir-i-Bakran was a Sufi
teacher in Linjan.

ASHTARJAN. Masjid-i-Jami

The Masjid-i-Jami at Ashtarjan, a village some
30 miles (48 km.) west of Isfahan, was built in
1315-16 (A.H. 715), by the order of
Muhammad ibn Mahmud ibn Ali al-Ashtarjani.
The inscription on the main portal identifies
Ahmad ibn Muhammad as the builder and
Hajji Muhammad as the tilecutter. Brick and
mortar of local origin were used in the
construction, so that the monument is in harmony
with the mud dwellings around it and appears to
grow out of them. The structural materials
of the mosque are hard fired. Designs
in plaster attract the eye, and color brightens
the drab masonry. Inside are the usual court and
domed chamber, but the variety and intricate
detail of the tile patterns give an
impression of novelty. The striving for verticality,
a characteristic of Il-Khanid builders, is well
exemplified in the soaring narrow façade. Each
of its components is designed to enhance
this effect, which is revealed most dramatically in
the height of the *iwan* arch, which is three times
its width.

PLATE 53

ASHTARJAN. Masjid-i-Jami

This calligraphy in the sanctuary *iwan* of the
Masjid-i-Jami at Ashtarjan is Naskhi writing in
turquoise tile, surrounded by carved stucco.
The script is a message from the Koran.
Although the Mongol conquerors retained their
nomadic way of life for many years—setting up
luxurious but temporary camps on the outskirts of
their cities—they were active builders by the end
of the 13th century. Ghazan Khan, the
predecessor of Oljeitu, announced his conversion
to the Moslem faith in 1295 and decreed soon
afterward that a mosque and a bath should
be erected in each community in his realm. He
specified that the revenues from the baths should be
allocated to the support of the religious centers.

PLATE **54**

NATANZ. *Khanaqah*

Two types of writing adorn the entrance façade
of the *khanaqah* at Natanz (built A.D. 1316;
A.H. 716). A cursive script on the left, *right*
in pink stucco, is contrasted with a rectangular
Kufic on the right. *left* Calligraphy was an esteemed
art in Islam, and the many versions of
script fostered a variety of designs.

PLATE 55

NATANZ. *Khanaqah* minaret

The shaft of the *khanaqah* minaret in Natanz
(A.D. 1324; A.H. 725) shows the adaptation of tile
and brick patterns to an extensive surface.
The glazed areas and the mortar are slightly recessed
so as to ensure a patterned effect even when the
sunlight does not shine on the enamel. The
minaret is 123 feet (37.5 m.) high and is
encircled by an inscription band of striking
vertical characters.

PLATE 56

NATANZ. Mausoleum of Shaykh Abd al-Samad al-Isfahani

The mausoleum of Shaykh Abd al-Samad al-Isfahani in Natanz (A.D. 1307; A.H. 707) is a small square chamber, about 19 feet across (5.95 m.) on the inside. Filtered light plays on the modeled white surfaces, adding depth to the dim recesses of the ceiling.

The complex at Natanz was built over a period of at least twenty years. The inferior design of some of the earlier buildings compared with the superb craftsmanship of the *khanaqah* façade has led Dr. Pope to state of the latter: " Much of its exceptional quality is probably due to workmen who were released from the tremendous constructions at Tabriz and Sultaniya."[1]

PLATE **57**

VARAMIN. Masjid-i-Jami

This detail is from the sanctuary portal of the
Masjid-i-Jami at Varamin (A.D. 1322-26;
A.H. 722-25). The formal geometric pattern lends
texture to the masonry and also acts as a foil for the
more elaborate surrounding decoration.
According to the inscription, Ali Qazvini was
the architect. The building was constructed under
the patronage of the last Il-Khanid ruler,
Abu Said.

PLATE 58

VARAMIN. Masjid-i-Jami

This view shows the interior of the dome, with
the zone of transition, in the Masjid-i-Jami
at Varamin. To create a place of devotion suitable
for large congregations yet sympathetic
to the individual daily worshiper was a
challenging problem for Moslem architects. In
Iran the outdoor court provided the solution for
large gatherings, while the small domed chamber
afforded seclusion for solitary prayer.
A vast horizontal space gives the individual
a feeling of loneliness, but a lofty dome can inspire
awe and exaltation within an intimate area.

It is interesting to compare the
architectural character of the Masjid-i-Jami in
Varamin with that of the northeast dome
chamber of the Masjid-i-Jami at Isfahan (Plate 10).
The zone of transition in the Varamin mosque
has the stronger horizontal lines of the two.
The dramatic focus on the dome is
developed first of all through the introduction of
color into the spandrels of the arches in the octagonal
zone, then through the addition of increased
light, which comes from the windows of the
sixteen-sided polygon. Lighting is unimportant in
the northeast dome chamber at Isfahan, but at
Varamin it is a vital factor. In both structures
the interior space is extremely vertical, and
interest ultimately culminates in the dome.
The Varamin dome is decorated with brick
patterns outlined in white and with insets
of Kufic writing.

CHAPTER III

Timurid Period

(A.D. 1380-1499; A.H. 781-904)

With the decline of the Il-Khanid regime, petty strife disrupted the land. The Muzaffarids in Isfahan maintained the high traditions of craftsmanship, but elsewhere little of note was constructed. After his conquest of Iran, Timur (Tamerlane) established a strong government which brought stability and prosperity to the area. This led to a cultural renaissance. Western historians have stressed the warlike and destructive character of the Timurids, but today the greater significance of these rulers lies in the fact that they were active patrons of the arts. Samarkand, Meshed and Herat are only a few of the cities that bear witness to their culture. Robert Byron, in discussing the originality of their taste, mentions that they sent to China for new ideas in painting. He writes: " These princes believed that to be a gentleman was to be, if not an artist oneself, at least a devotee of the arts."[1]

The Timurid desire for magnificence resulted in an era of grandiose buildings. Tall, bulbous domes adorned many mosques and *madrasas*, particularly in the neighborhood of Samarkand, the capital. Frequently, in Iran and Afghanistan, the towering *iwan* dominated the composition. Color was used lavishly, to give an effect of brilliance as well as to accent structure and architectural proportions. Religious buildings, including minarets, were sometimes faced entirely with glazed tile. Floral patterns occurred frequently in the mosaic work, and the range of colors increased.

PLATE **59**

HERAT. Husein Bayqara *madrasa*

In Herat white marble was often employed as a framing for the tile designs (an innovation which came from India). In the time of the Timurid prince Husein Bayqara, Herat was a cultural center of renown, famous for its poets and miniaturists, as well as its architects and ceramists. Babur, a descendant of Timur, visited the town during this period and wrote a glowing account of it in his memoirs.[2]

The shaft of this minaret from the Husein Bayqara *madrasa* (A.D. 1469-1506; A.H. 873-911) in Herat is almost 150 feet (about 45 m.) high.

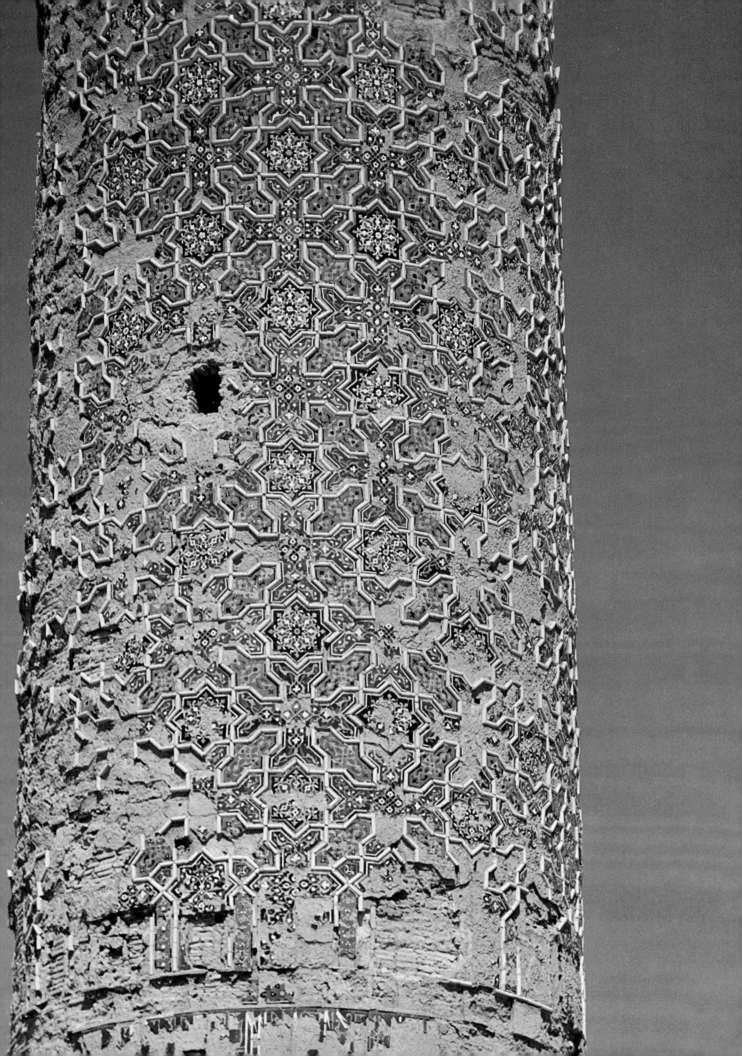

PLATE 60

HERAT. Mausoleum of Gawhar Shad

The mausoleum of Gawhar Shad was built at
Herat in 1417-32 (A.H. 820-35). Fluting on the
dome reflects sunlight from many facets and
accentuates the brilliance of the tiles. The architect
of this tomb was most probably Qavam ad-Din,
of Shiraz, the designer of the Gawhar Shad
mosque in Meshed and the original
architect of the Khargird *madrasa* (Plates 70-74).
Gawhar Shad, daughter-in-law of Timur, was
a lavish patroness of religious art. Unfortunately,
many of her monuments in Herat were destroyed
in 1885, among them her mosque and
madrasa, which were demolished by the British
to hinder a Russian advance. One minaret
and the mausoleum are all that remain. A British
officer writing in August 1885, describes those
lost monuments:

"These are ruins of distinct buildings (the *masjid* and the
madrasa) each with its central dome, flanked by high
square-built wings, enclosing a gigantic court in front.
The entrance to the court is below an arch, which forms
by far the most prominent feature. These main
arches must be at least 80 feet high; and as a high square
wall is carried up above the crown to the height of
another 40 feet or so, this arched entrance dwarfs by
its enormous size both the dome and the delicate forms
of the four minarets which guard the building at
each corner, and which are in themselves marvelously
beautiful in outline and symmetry. The face and
interior of the *masalla* [sic] (except the wings), as well as
the exterior of the minarets, and of the domed
masjid which stands apart, covering the shrine of
Shah Rukh, are all covered with enamel-work illustrating
the delicate beauty of an art which is lost. Shades of
blue and green, azure and emerald, to the deep
tones of indigo and of a lustrous peacock green, varied
with yellows from lemon to russet, including
all the tints of dying and dead leaves in autumn, are
blended in the devices of the faience." [1]

PLATE **61**

GAZUR GAH. Sanctuary of Abd Allah Ansari

Old men sun themselves in the entrance portal
of the sanctuary of Abd Allah Ansari, at
Gazur Gah (near Herat). Rebuilt by Shah Rukh in
1428 (A.H. 832), the quiet charm of the shrine
reflects the spirit of the saint, mystic and
poet to whom the structure is dedicated. Ansari
died in 1090, but his verse is well remembered.

My friend, see thine own faults;
The faults of others,
For thee they are not.
Make thy heart forgiving;
Nor sell thy soul for the fruits of the world.

It is wrong to consider oneself above all others
And to exalt one's self
Learn from the pupil of thine eye
To see others, but to thyself be blind.

Know friend,
Human sorrow springs from three things:
To want before it is due,
To want more than the destined share,
To want for oneself
What belongs to others.

Abdullah Ansari, "Springs of Human Sorrows"[1]

PLATE 62

GAZUR GAH. Sanctuary of Abd Allah Ansari

The fine tile work of the sanctuary of
Abd Allah Ansari dates from the period of
Shah Rukh, son of Timur. The example seen here
is a mosaic tile panel on the west wall of
the inner court. Extreme brilliance was achieved
with mosaic tile, as each color was fired at the ideal
temperature for that particular glaze. The
design was carefully chipped from square tiles
baked in their individual colors. Less arduous was
a system of painting square tiles with portions
of the design and then assembling
the squares. However, with this method
(haft rangi) some perfection of color was
sacrificed. Shah Abbas I, who wished to have his
vast monuments faced with tile as quickly as
possible, often favored the haft rangi technique.

PLATE **63**

GAZUR GAH. Sanctuary of Abd Allah Ansari

This detail is from a panel on the entrance façade
of the sanctuary of Ansari. Here the mortar
has been covered with royal-blue faience.
A Moslem tradition forbidding the representation of
living creatures in holy places, though not
always followed, restricted the choice of
subject matter. Foliage, flowers, stars
and geometric patterns predominate in the designs.
This composition of a vase filled with flowers
would have been especially appealing to a
desert people. A highly sophisticated abstraction,
with no attempt at naturalism, is seen here.

PLATE **64**

GAZUR GAH. Sanctuary of Abd Allah Ansari

This mosaic faience panel from the Ansari shrine is in the court, to the left of the sanctuary *iwan*. The harlequin pattern was very popular with Timurid ceramists and occurs often on the monuments of Samarkand and Bukhara. The serpentine movement of white tiles through the stylized flower motifs lends a pleasing freedom to a narrow symmetrical design.

GAZUR GAH. Sanctuary of Abd Allah Ansari

The principal *iwan* of this shrine is approximately 70 feet (about 21 m.) high. The border of this lower panel from the northeast side of the *iwan* has a bold, mobile pattern which contrasts with the linear designs within. A raised molding outlines the rectangular sections with their Kufic inscriptions. They are arranged to make the panel less stiff and to give emphasis to the central plaque. The prevalence of peach tones is unusual.

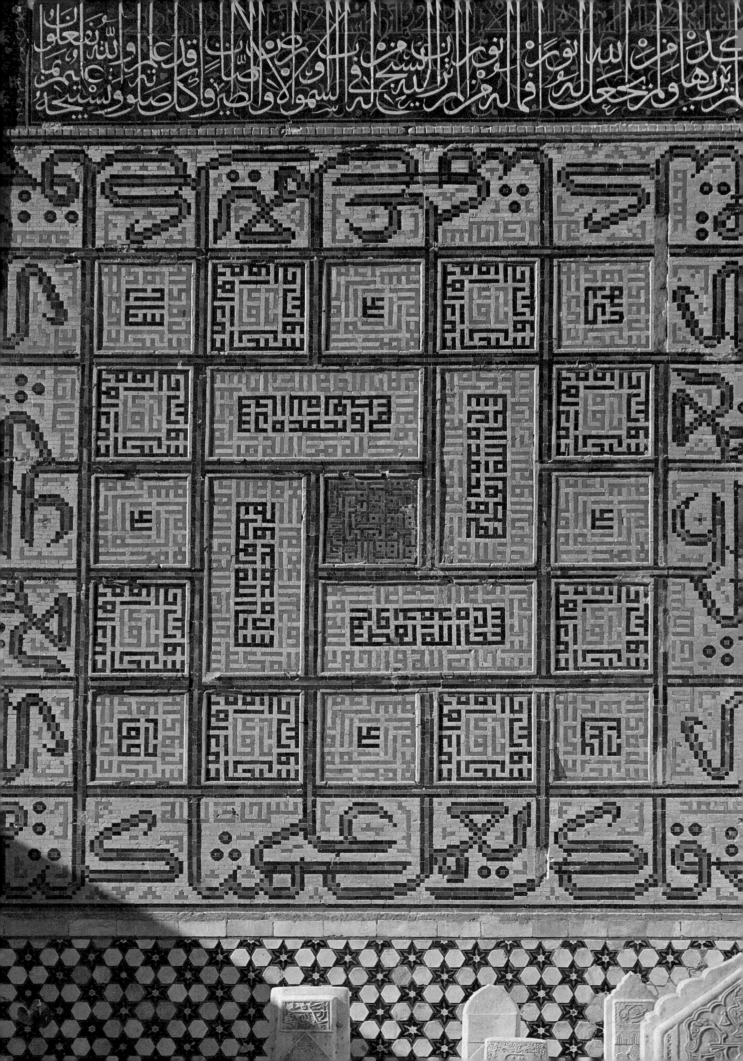

GAZUR GAH. Sanctuary of Abd Allah Ansari

This panel in the Ansari shrine is just above the one depicted in Plate 65. The raised squares containing floral motifs give the illusion of random scattering, an illusion which is enhanced by the use of rhombuses, triangles and hexagons in the background. The artistic relations between the Timurids and the Chinese are apparent in the distribution of the seal-like rhombuses, with their writing. This oriental influence is seen also in some of the panels of the Blue Mosque at Tabriz (Plate 77).

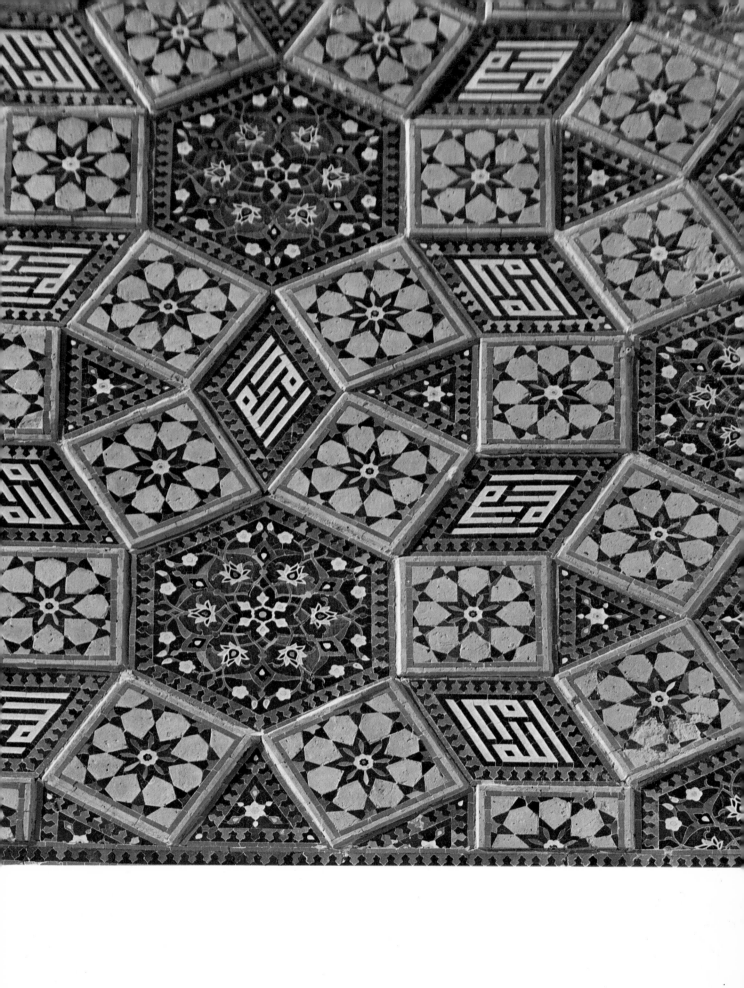

KHARGIRD. Neighboring village

A typical village, dun-colored and stark, huddles
on the eastern edge of the Great Salt Desert,
near Khargird. Bred in austerity, Iranians are
deeply responsive to an abundant Nature.
Luxuriant, twining vines and the
glorious extravagance of flowers symbolize the
precious gift of fertility. Just as Iranian religious
architecture is decorated with designs of
foliage and blossoms, so Iranian poetry is often
devoted to gardens.

'Twas morning, and the Lord of day
Had shed his light o'er Shiraz' towers,
Where bulbuls trill their love-lorn lay
To serenade the maiden flowers.

Like them, oppressed by love's sweet pain,
I wander in a garden fair;
And there, to cool my throbbing brain,
I woo the perfumed morning air.

The damask rose with beauty gleams,
Its face all bathed in ruddy light,
And shines like some bright star that beams
From out the somber veil of night.

Hafiz, "Lesson of the Flowers"[1]

PLATE **68**

TURBAT-I-SHAYKH JAM. Masjid-i-Kali

The Masjid-i-Kali at Turbat-i-Shaykh Jam
(inscribed date is A.H. 844 [A.D. 1440]) was
the work of the architect Ustad Hajji Mahmud-i-
Zayn. In the court, blind arches accent the
majestic west portal, and a dome rises above the wall
to form a composition utterly satisfying
in its rhythm and proportion. Surrounded by
the drab and the bleak, desert people
crave color. Numerous variations of blue tile and
buff brick culminate in the vibrant turquoise of
the dome.

PLATE **69**

TURBAT-I-SHAYKH JAM. Masjid-i-Kali

This stucco *mihrab* (mid-14th century
[mid-8th century A.H.]) in the Sufi oratory of the
Masjid-i-Kali at Turbat-i-Shaykh Jam is
signed: " The work of the weak, poor slave, who
puts his hopes in the mercy of the mighty Lord,
Khwaja Zaki ibn Muhammad ibn Mas'ud-i-Kirmani."
A rich profusion of flowers and vines
turns the thoughts of the worshiper
from the aridity of his surroundings to the bounty
of the heavens. Oriented toward Mecca, the
mihrab is conceived of as the glorious door to
another world.

Connected with the Masjid-i-Kali is the
mausoleum of Ahmad-ibn-Allah Hasan, a
renowned Sufi saint and teacher who died in 1141
(A.H. 536). Some of the structures in the
complex may date from the Seljuk period.
Dr. D. N. Wilber dates the Sufi oratory at about
1333 (about A.H. 733), on stylistic grounds
as well as on the fact that the doors to the hall are
inscribed with this date.[1]

PLATE **70**

KHARGIRD. *Madrasa*

The northeast elevation of the *madrasa* at
Khargird (A.D. 1444-45; A.H. 848) is
seen here. The building was designed and begun by
Qavam ad-Din, who died before the structure
was completed. The work was finished by
Ghiyath ad-Din. Qavam ad-Din was Shah Rukh's
chief architect and the domed chamber to the
left of the entrance portal should probably be
attributed to him (Plate 73). Although much of it is
in ruins, this school of theology remains
one of the great structures of the Timurid period.
The beige bricks give the building the appearance
of having grown from the soil around it,
while the royal- and light-blue tiles of the
dignified façade harmonize with the purple
mountains. The exterior measures 138 by 184 feet
(42 by 56 m.), and despite a lofty entrance *iwan*,
a horizontal effect prevails. Khargird, which
is located in eastern Iran, about two miles (or about
three kilometers) from Khaf, is today nearly
deserted, but in the 10th century (4th century A.H.)
it was an important town. The region
was well irrigated and was noted particularly
for its silk, pomegranates, and grapes.

PLATE **71**

KHARGIRD. *Madrasa*

This detail from the *madrasa* at Khargird is
in the arch of the main entrance. To the right of
the portal an inscription reads: " By the endeavors
of the feeble slave Khwaja Rayhan ibn Ahmad."
According to A. U. Pope, he was probably
the ceramist.[1] The placement of the Kufic
plaques is reminiscent of that in the Ansari shrine
at Gazur Gah (Plate 66), which was completed
some seventeen years earlier.

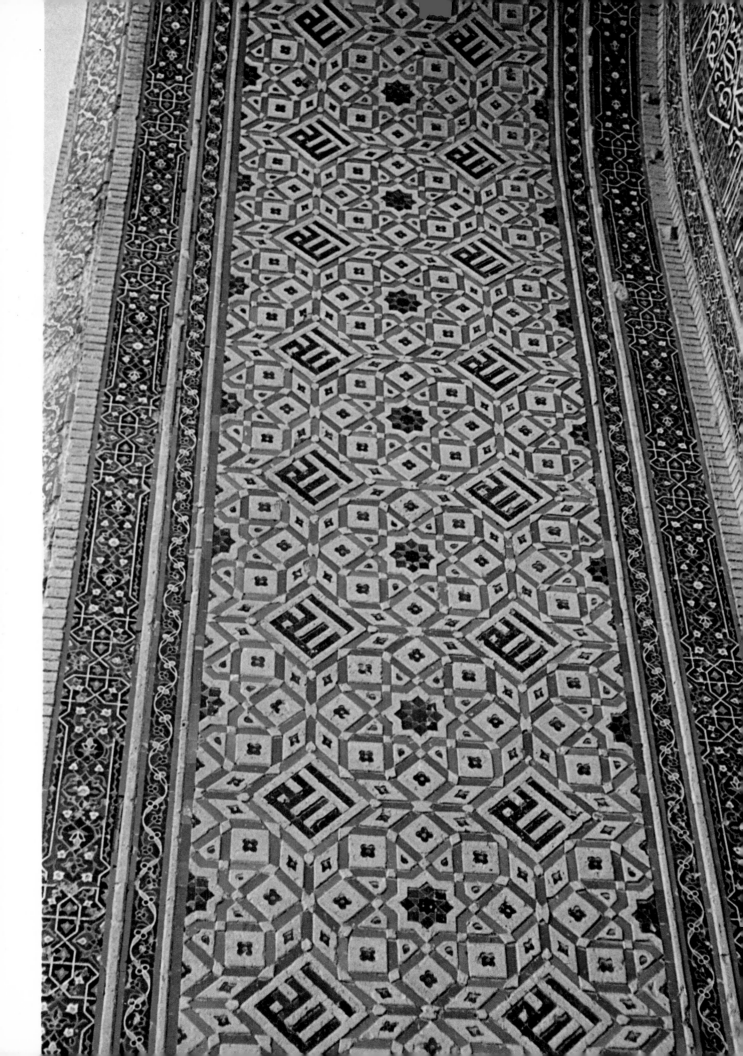

PLATE **72**

KHARGIRD. *Madrasa*

A blind arch at the southwest corner illustrates
one version of the patterns which appear on
the entire façade of the Khargird *madrasa*. These
designs are executed in two shades of blue glaze on
a background of natural brick. Originally
madrasas were private schools devoted to religious
studies. By the end of the 11th century, the
scope of their curriculum had been broadened to
include many secular disciplines. The
term *madrasa* stems from the Arab word *darasa*,
which means to study or to read.

KHARGIRD. *Madrasa*

This interior view of the Khargird *madrasa* shows
the walls and dome of the northeast chamber;
the brick facing of the exterior second dome appears
near the top of the illustration. The
simplicity of white, and the fact that structural
elements play an important role in the decoration,
bring order and dignity to the intricate
composition. This chamber has a double drum as
well as the two domes. Between the drums is a
gallery. The same construction occurs
in the Gawhar Shad Mausoleum (Plate 60), but there
a tall third dome, covered with mosaic tile,
completes the exterior. Whether such a third
dome was considered for Khargird is open to
question. Qavam ad-Din employed similar vaulting
systems for the interiors of the Gawhar Shad
tomb and the Khargird *madrasa*. One
difference in the latter building is that,
as Robert Byron points out, ". . . a ring of stalactite
niches intervenes before the octagon, above which
stand eight flattened stilted windows
giving on to the gallery between the drums. The
dome itself rests on small pendentives, which
spring from clusters of ribs between the windows."[2]

KHARGIRD. *Madrasa*

Stalactites with painted designs in pastel colors
adorn a corner squinch in the northwest chamber.
This room was probably the work of
Ghiyath ad-Din, the successor to Qavam ad-Din.
Both architects were natives of Shiraz.
Although " stalactites " is the usual term in
English for this type of work the more descriptive
expression " honeycomb " is sometimes used.
The decorative function of stalactite work was to fill
in the deep recess of an arch, most particularly
of a squinch. Stalactites were not used at
Sangbast (Plates 2 and 3) or in the northeast dome
chamber at Isfahan (Plate 10), but by the
15th century they had become a favorite device of
architects.

TABRIZ. Blue Mosque

The Blue Mosque (Masjid-i-Kabud) at Tabriz was
built in 1465 (A.H. 870), under the patronage of
Saliha Khanun, daughter of Jahanshah.
The architect, according to an inscription in the
entrance portal (opposite) was Nimat Allah ibn
Muhammad Bawvab. Although blue predominates
in this building, the harmonious intermingling
of rich gold and brown and olive green brings a
special character to the decoration of the
mosque. Only fragments of the tilework remain,
but they exemplify the finest
color, composition and craftsmanship in glazed
adornment. A façade 170 feet (52 m.) long
terminated in round bastions, which were
surmounted by very tall minarets. The
center chambers and halls were domed in this unique
example of a completely covered mosque in Iran.
The elimination of the open court may be
attributed to the severe winter climate of Tabriz.

Tabriz has had a turbulent history and has been
occupied by Arabs, Seljuks, Ottomans
and Russians. The conquerors Genghis Khan and
Timur did heavy damage to Tabriz, but their
descendants did much to glorify the city. Later,
Tabriz had a strong influence on the art
of other regions. After capturing the city in 1514,
the Ottoman Sultan Selim I imported three
thousand craftsmen from Tabriz to decorate his
monuments in Turkey.

In the 15th century Tabriz was the largest city in
the world (outside of China) and had a population
of about one and a quarter million. The
revenues Timur received from the town exceeded
those of the King of France. Sir Thomas Herbert,
visiting in 1683, wrote: " Tabriz is great
and well peopled with a large bazaar and lovely
gardens." [1] Forty-three years later,
Chardin commented: " The piazza of Tauris
[Tabriz] is the most spacious piazza that ever I saw
in any city of the world, and far surpasses
that of Ispahan [Isfahan]." [2]

PLATE **76**

TABRIZ. Blue Mosque

These panels, located to the right in the entrance
portal of the Blue Mosque, have a floral pattern,
in buff stucco, embroidered over the faience
tilework. A slight relief and contrasting
textures add interest to the pattern and to the Kufic
script. (The section between the panels, being
much damaged, has been cropped from
the photograph.)

PLATE **77**

TABRIZ. Blue Mosque

A subtle pattern in blue and gold covers the surface
of this panel on the south wall of the entrance
to the sanctuary chamber. Several styles of
calligraphy appear in the design. Especially
noteworthy is the upper band of Kufic.

PLATE 78

TABRIZ. Blue Mosque

In the domed corridor which partially surrounds
the main chamber this dado of black-and-white
tilework provides a strong base for the
elaborate wall decoration. Minute royal-blue
rhombuses within the white lines add a subtle touch
of color. This style of geometric dado is
frequently found in 15th– and 16th–century
Ottoman buildings.

CHAPTER IV **Safavid
Period**

(A.D. 1499-1736; A.H. 994-1149)

Until the reign of Shah Abbas I (A.D. 1587-1628;
A.H. 996-1037) Safavid design was essentially
a continuation of Timurid design and
was preoccupied chiefly with the increasing refine-
ment of mosaic detail. Shah Abbas, as Pope
says, " revived the tradition of building
in the grand manner . . . and reaffirmed the Iranian
ideals of the planned city and imperial
magnificence expressed in architecture." [1] Major
religious monuments were completely faced
inside and out with polychrome tile. Mosaic
faience of fine quality was produced, but
after 1616 the more rapid, though less brilliant,
technique of painted tiles *(haft rangi)* was
frequently employed. Usually the double dome
was preferred, but whichever form was selected
there was greater stress on the balance
of the composition, with neither dome nor *iwan* being
allowed to dominate.

   Shah Abbas I, a contemporary of
Queen Elizabeth of England, Henry IV and
Louis XIII of France, and Akbar in India, was an
outstanding monarch. A successful general and a
strong administrator, he was also keenly
interested in the commercial welfare and artistic
creativity of his country. Early in his
reign he moved his capital to Isfahan, and shortly
thereafter he transformed the town into
a city of incredible splendor—a city of gardens,
broad avenues lined with palaces, and glittering
mosques.

ISFAHAN. *Maidan*

The *Maidan* at Isfahan was constructed between
1597 and 1617 (A.H. 1006-26). It measures
1674 by 540 feet (512 by 159 m.). Each of the
four principal edifices on it has been built on a
different side of the rectangle, which is also
surrounded by a two-story arcade. On the right is the
Ali Kapu, which served as the seat of
of government and as a royal palace used for
entertaining. At the far end of the
plaza is the Masjid-i-Shah. Opposite the Ali Kapu
is the Masjid-i-Shaykh Lutfullah (Plate 96),
and facing the Masjid-i-Shah is the entrance portal
to the bazaar, from which this photograph
was taken.

Sir Thomas Herbert, writing in 1638,
compared the *maidan* to the Royal Exchequer [sic]
in London and the Place Royale in Paris but
admitted that the Isfahan plaza was six
times as large as these. He stated: " The Mydan
or Great Market is without doubt the
most spacious, pleasant, and Aromatick Market in
the Universe." [2] André Godard, writing three
hundred years later, says: " As to his [Shah Abbas']
town, it is above all a plan, with lines and
masses and sweeping perspectives—a magnificent
concept born half a century before Versailles." [3]

ISFAHAN. Masjid-i-Shah

The Masjid-i-Shah at Isfahan was built between
1612 and 1638 (A.H. 1021-48) by Abu'l Qasim,
under the patronage of Shah Abbas I. The entrance
portal (shown here), which was completed
in 1616 (A.H. 1025), is 90 feet (27.5 m.) high.
Despite the brilliance of the Safavid decoration,
basic structural elements predominate.

ISFAHAN. Masjid-i-Shah

A panel with paired peacocks adorns the entrance
portal of the Masjid-i-Shah. The façades
of the buildings on the *maidan* at Isfahan are
decorated in mosaic faience. The panel
shown here is interesting not only for its artistic
merits but also because the Moslem proscription of
the depiction of living creatures has been
violated in a royal mosque.

PLATE 82

ISFAHAN. Masjid-i-Shah

The view opposite shows the sanctuary *iwan* and
ablution pool of the Masjid-i-Shah. Only the
Kufic inscriptions are mosaic faience; all the other
surfaces of the enclosed court are of painted
tiles. The interior of the dome is 117 feet
(about 35 m.) high.

The dramatic effect of the sanctuary chamber is
enhanced by the fact that it was necessary
to change the angle of approach within
the entrance area. The portal faces north onto the
Maidan, but the mosque proper had to be
oriented to the southwest, toward Mecca.

Figure G. Plan of the Masjid-i-Shah, Isfahan.

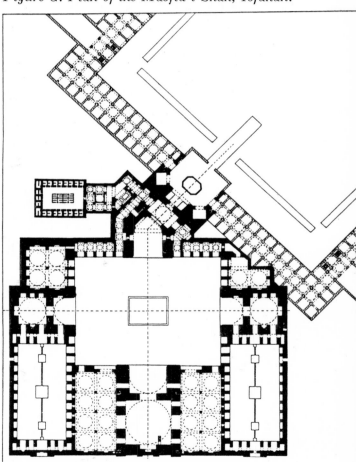

PLATE 83

ISFAHAN. Masjid-i-Jami

This view shows the court of the Masjid-i-Jami,
Isfahan. On the left is the southwest
or sanctuary *iwan* and the roof of the domed
chamber of Nizam al-Mulk; on the right is the
northwest *iwan*.

(see color plate on following two pages)

PLATE **84**

ISFAHAN. Masjid-i-Jami

Originally built *circa* 1121-22 (A.H. 515) in
the Seljuk period, the northwest *iwan* of the
Masjid-i-Jami was redecorated 1700-01
(A.H. 1112), in the reign of Shah Sultan Husayn,
under the direction of Hajji Kasem.

The colossal *iwan* originated in eastern
Iran and was probably brought west by the
Parthians on their trek from Khurasan.
The Sassanians later combined the monumental arch
with deep barrel vaulting to create
impressive palaces such as Ctesiphon. The *iwan*
persisted as a place of prayer in eastern Iran
in the form of the *musalla*, a tall structure oriented
toward Mecca. Even with the inclusion
of a domed chamber in a mosque the emphasis
in the east was for a long time on the
great *iwan* rather than the dome.

It was in Khurasan, too, that the *madrasa*
originated. During the Seljuk period this building,
with its typical plan of an enclosed court and four
iwans, spread rapidly westward. Meanwhile,
in western Iran, Arab edifices in nearby Damascus
and Baghdad influenced the development of the
domed chamber as a mosque. The fusion of these
different architectural concepts produced the
typical Iranian Mosque—a closed court with four
monumental *iwans* and a domed sanctuary
chamber.

PLATE **85**

ISFAHAN. Masjid-i-Jami

The panel shown here is from the northwest *iwan*
o˚ the Masjid-i-Jami. Beneath a frieze of script
containing a quotation from the Koran
a design in low relief of trapeziums around a diamond,
stands out against a delicate geometric pattern.

PLATE **86**

ISFAHAN. Masjid-i-Jami

In this mosaic faience panel in the northwest *iwan*,
dainty motifs in light blue with touches of
clear yellow characterize 18th–century decoration.

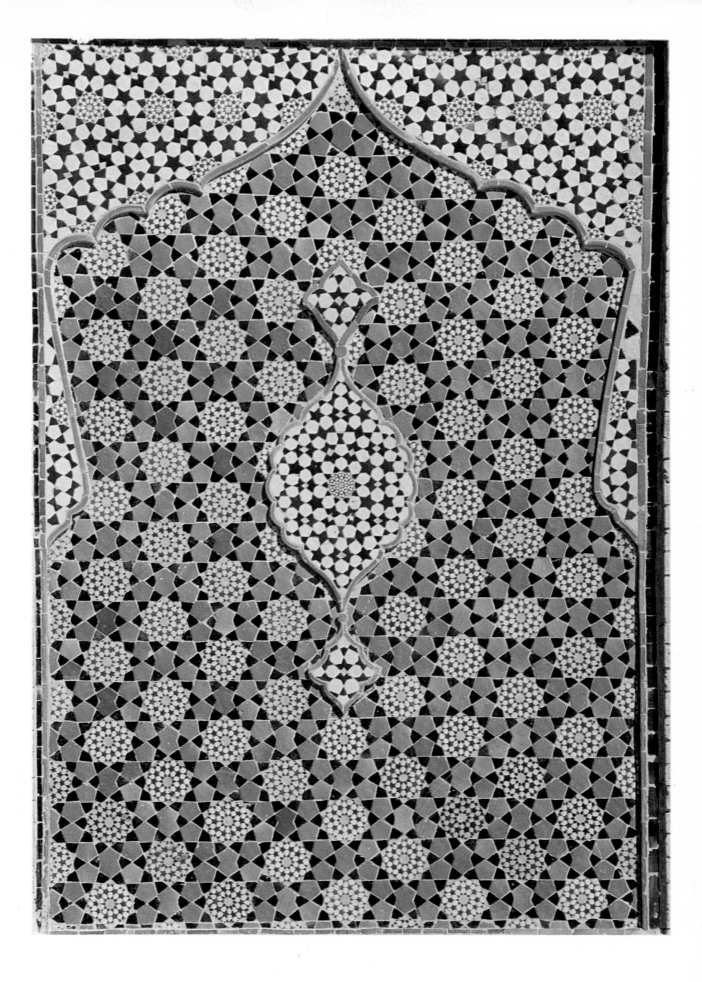

ISFAHAN. Masjid-i-Jami

This panel from the southwest *iwan* of the
Masjid-i-Jami dates from 1475-76 (A.H. 880) which
makes it over two hundred years earlier than the
panels in the northwest *iwan* (Plates 85 and 86).
Although strictly symmetrical, the design
avoids monotony through the use of a variety of
shapes in the raised plaques. This work
was done under the orders of Ak-Koyunlu
Abu'l-Nasr Bahadur (better known as Uzun
Hasan). He sponsored much remodeling of the
Jami, including the decoration of the façades of the
court with mosaic faience.

PLATE **88**

ISFAHAN. Harun-i-Vilaya mausoleum

This view, taken from the court, shows the
entrance portal and part of the façade of the
Harun-i-Vilaya mausoleum in Isfahan.
Built in 1513 (A.H. 918), during the reign of the first
Safavid ruler, Shah Ismail I, this tomb is
inscribed as being the " work of the poor mason,
Husayn." The varying proportions of
the arches and depths of the recesses create a
rhythmic composition. Above the Kufic inscription
in the *iwan*, peacocks face each other
within a frame of Chinese cloud bands.

PLATE **89**

ISFAHAN. Harun-i-Vilaya mausoleum

Mosaic faience is set with a jeweler's precision
in the entrance portal of the Harun-i-Vilaya tomb.
Flowers grow in graceful profusion from
a vase—symbolizing the gifts of Nature emerging
from the Waters of Life. It was not only
poets and artists who were fascinated with plants,
for the Koran itself extols the blessings of the
heavenly Tree of Abundance.

PLATE 90

ISFAHAN. Darb-i-Kushk

Detail of a mosaic tile panel in the entrance portal
of the Darb-i-Kushk, an oratory in the
Kushk district of Isfahan. It was erected
1496-97 (A.H. 902) by Zin al-Dawle wal-Seadet
wal-Din during the reign of Abu'l Muzaffar Rustam
Bahadur Khan, grandson of Uzun Hasan.
This portal has been reconstructed in the garden
of the Chehel Sutun. The stylization of the dahlias,
particularly of their outer border, makes
their Iranian name, " star flower," more
comprehensible. Various flora and fauna are often
charmingly intermingled in Iranian terminology.
For instance, the song of the nightingale is
the " flower cry " *(gulbang)*. [1]

PLATE **91**

ISFAHAN. Chehel Sutun

The Chehel Sutun (Palace of the Forty Columns)
was built by Shah Abbas I at Isfahan in 1611
(A.H. 1020). Painted designs on the ceiling and along
the overhang brighten the dark wood. Slender
supporting columns of chanar trunks
contrast with the mass of the roof. Tracing its
architectural descent from the Achaemenian Hall of
a Hundred Columns at Persepolis and the *iwan*
frame for the thrones in the Sassanian
palaces, the Chehel Sutun also reflects the
Iranian love of color and of the out-of-doors.

When the palace was used for court receptions,
the floor was covered with rugs, and brilliantly
colored curtains were hung between the
columns and extended outward as awnings. A
contemporary description by a European traveler
describes the festivities of a royal party:

Then the dancing wenches went to work, first throwing
off their loose garments or vests—the other was close
to the body resembling trousers, but of several pieces of
satin of sundry colors; their hair was long and
dangling in curls; about their faces hung ropes of
pearls, and about their wrists and legs were wreathed
golden bracelets with bells, which, with the cymbals and
timbrels in their hands, made the best concert. Their
dancing was not after the usual manner, for each of
them kept within a small circle and made, as it
were, every limb dance in order after each other, even to
admiration.[1]

PLATE 92

ISFAHAN. Ali Kapu

This fresco is on the ceiling of the main reception hall of the Ali Kapu, Isfahan. Originally a Timurid structure, the Ali Kapu was restored by Shah Ismail and renovated completely by Shah Abbas I from 1598 to about 1612 (A.H. 1006–*circa* 1025). Sir Thomas Herbert attended an audience at the Ali Kapu and wrote the following description in 1638: " Within the rooms are arched, enlightened by curious trellises, the roof imbossed with red, blue, white and gold, the sides with painted sports and Painted Images, the ground spread with rich and curious carpets of silk and gold, without other furniture." [1]

Ali kapu means " high door " and has the same connotation of royal authority as does " Sublime Porte " in Turkey. The Ali Kapu was both for official receptions and as a seat of government. Petitions were brought by citizens and left at the door for the Shah's consideration. Aggrieved subjects paraded outside the entrance, rending their clothing and wailing until the monarch sent out to inquire as to their complaints. Chardin, in the 17th century, saw many such demonstrations. Peasants, especially, came bearing samples of their withered crops to request a lessening of their taxes.

An Italian team is at present completely restoring the Ali Kapu and intends to publish a full photographic record of the frescoes.

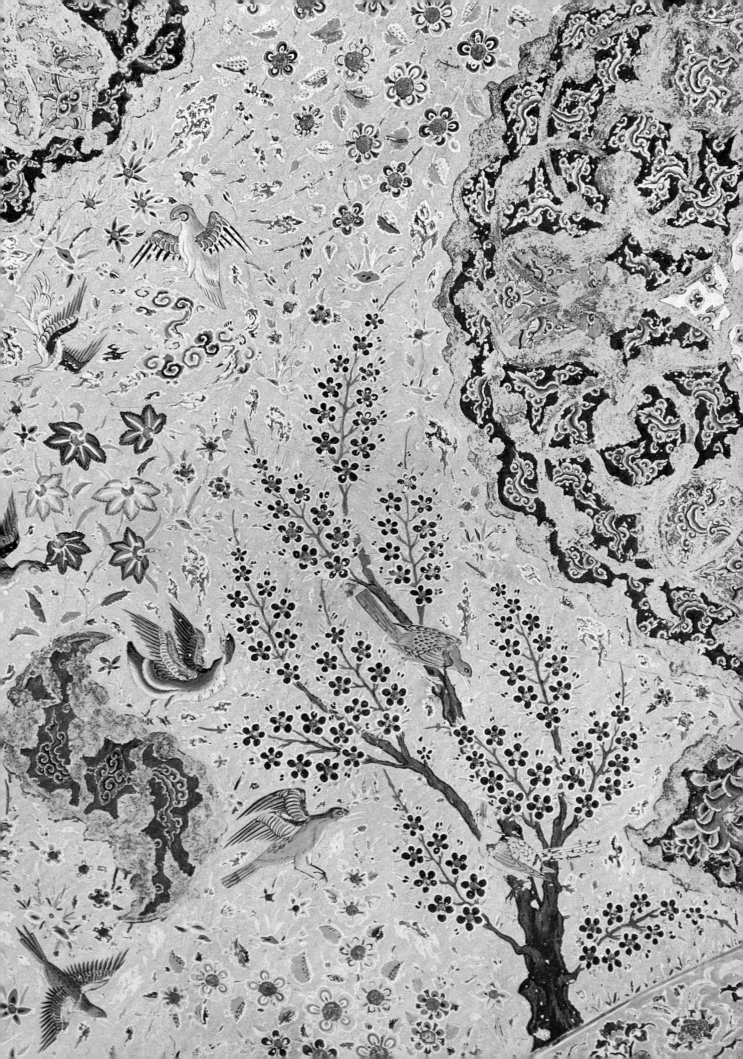

ISFAHAN. Hesht Behest

Figure H. The Hesht Behest, Isfahan, exterior, drawing by P. Coste.

The Hesht Behest (Palace of the Eight Paradises) is an octagonal structure, typical of many royal palaces in Isfahan. Commissioned by Shah Suleyman, it was built about 1669 (about A.H. 1081). These mid-19th century drawings by Coste depict the façade of the building and the interior of the central hall. The garden, visible at all times through the great arches, is an integral part of the structure. The domed ceiling of the main reception room is painted in purple on a glittering gold base, while above the windows, in the lantern dome, fragments of mirror sparkle in the light.

Figure I. The Hesht Behest, Isfahan, interior, drawing by P. Coste.

ISFAHAN. Hesht Behest

Painted tile designs of birds, animals, and hunting scenes, found on the spandrels of the outer blind arches, enliven the façades of the Hesht Behest in Isfahan.

Hunting was a favorite pastime of the Shahs. Seven days before the court's departure for a hunting trip the tents, rugs, gold services, and other prerequisites for the camp were sent off. From five to seven thousand camels were needed to transport this equipage. The splendor of these hunting camps may be judged from the fact that each nobleman was allotted some five hundred square feet for his tent. Under the silk-lined canopies were rooms for his harem, a bath, and a reception hall. The interiors were carpeted, strewn with soft cushions and draped in shimmering brocades. Pools and waterways adorned the site, and flowers blossomed in these " gardens for a day or two."

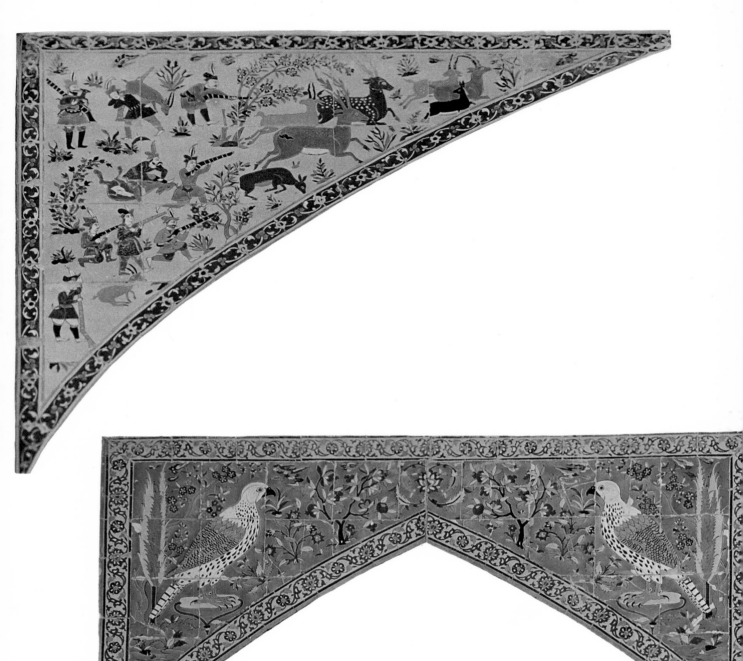

PLATE 95

ISFAHAN. Hesht Behest

The ceiling in a second floor reception room of
the Hesht Behest glistens with mirror decoration.
Chardin, writing in 1676, was enchanted by the
Hesht Behest.

When one walks in this place expressly made for the
delights of love, and when one passes through all
these cabinets and niches, one's heart is melted to such an
extent that, to speak candidly, one always leaves
with a very ill grace. The climate without doubt
contributes much towards exciting this amorous
disposition; but assuredly these places, although in
some respects little more than cardboard castles, are
nevertheless more smiling and agreeable than our most
sumptuous palaces.[1]

ISFAHAN. Masjid-i-Shaykh Lutfullah

The Masjid-i-Shaykh Lutfullah in Isfahan was
built by Shah Abbas I, between 1601 and
1618 (A.H. 1011-28), in honor of his father-in-law.
The architect was Muhammad Rida ibn Ustad
Husayn, and the calligraphy was executed by
Ali Reza. The portal of this mosque, like that of the
Masjid-i-Shah, faces the *Maidan* (but on the
east side). Inside, a tiled corridor has
been designed to go around the left side of the
domed chamber and so to enter this
sanctuary directly opposite the *mihrab*, which is
in the wall oriented toward Mecca.

Seen from the front of the building, the dome
rises off center to the portal with a pleasing
effect. Luxuriant vines adorn this hemisphere and
give the impression, against the desert
color, of a bountiful Nature. Being a single-shell
structure, the dome from the exterior appears low,
but inside the restricted space of the
sanctuary chamber it seems very high. Early
Iranian domes were normally single-shell structures.
As large masonry domes should decrease in
thickness toward the top, this presented a problem.
At the base a vault would often be
three bricks thick. The thickness would then
be reduced until, at the summit, it was
only one and a half bricks. This technique
produced a jagged contour. The steps on the outer
surface of the dome were usually smoothed
by a covering of dressed brick. Another problem
arose with the desire for a more imposing
exterior height. Interiors became disproportionately
lofty; hence the double dome, which permitted
an aesthetically pleasing adjustment of
the interior space, was invented. The double
dome also provided a new solution to the problem of
the stepped outer surface: the inner dome
was constructed as before, with a smooth interior
and rough exterior; the outer shell was
now built with a smooth contour, and the steps
were left on its concave inner side, facing the
unfinished surface of the lower dome.[1]

ISFAHAN. Masjid-i-Shaykh Lutfullah

The mosaic tile designs on the interior walls of
the Masjid-i-Shaykh Lutfullah are scaled to the
great arches yet are perfect to the most
minute detail. The vivid turquoise of the cable
molding is repeated in the color harmony
of the interior—as a rosette in the apex of the dome,
and as a sheet of blue in the tiled floor. Because
a mosque seeks to draw the thoughts
of a worshiper away from the everyday material
world, the self-contained quality of this
chamber is significant. No views of other halls or of
the out-of-doors detracts from its seclusion. The
only entrance opens onto a narrow tiled
corridor, and all the windows are high double grilles.

PLATE 98

ISFAHAN. Masjid-i-Shaykh Lutfullah

The dome and zone of transition of the
Masjid-i-Shaykh Lutfullah are shown here. The
diameter of the dome is 42 feet (12.80 m.). A
turquoise cable outlines the arches and squinches, but
structure has renounced its primacy to
decoration. The intellectual beauty of the
northeast dome chamber in the nearby Masjid-i-
Jami stands, as Byron says, " at the opposite
pole to the Mosque of Sheikh Lutfullah
[which] is Persian in the fabulous sense. No
European can previously have had any idea that
abstract pattern was capable of so profound
a splendor. It is a richness of light and surface, of
pattern and color only." [2]

PLATE **99**

ISFAHAN. *Madrasa* Mader-i-Shah

The dome and minaret of the *Madrasa*
Mader-i-Shah are shown here. This last monument
of the Safavids marks the end of the era of
the great contributions of Islamic Iran and
Afghanistan to architecture and design.
A backward glance over the seven hundred years
which separate the stark brick tower of the
Gunbad-i-Kabus and the resplendent dome and
minaret of the Mader-i-Shah *Madrasa*,
shows vistas of search and invention, of challenge
and fruition.

The structural potentialities of brick were
evaluated, in creations which ranged from soaring
towers to great arches. The transition
from square chamber to domed ceiling was
tentatively explored in 11th–century Sangbast and
dynamically expressed some fifty years later in the
northeast dome chamber at Isfahan; it
reached a new aesthetic interpretation in the
gleaming sophistication of the Lutfullah. Brick, so
rigorously structural at the outset, developed a
wealth of design patterns at Kharraqan and finally
bequeathed its motifs to the new craft of
mosaic faience.

Color, an exotic accent in the Gunbad-i-Surkh,
was used in impressive harmony with brick on the
façades at Khargird, became a series of
iridescent pictures in the mosaics of the Ansari
shrine and evolved into a blazing mantle for the
Masjid-i-Shah.

Light and shadow provided a subtle relief
which lent interest to great wall areas and,
at times, extended to the sphere of dramatic
interpretation (at Varamin and Khargird, and in
the impressionism of Natanz).

The use of counterbalanced forms to create new
harmonies more challenging than strict symmetry
found expression in mosques at Turbat-i-Shaykh
Jam and Isfahan.

Figure J. View of the Chahar Bagh and the Madrasa Mader-i-Shah, Isfahan, by P. Coste.

This drawing, made by Coste in 1867 (A.H. 1283), shows the avenue of the Chahar Bagh and the *Madrasa* Mader-i-Shah in Isfahan. The *madrasa* was erected by the mother of Shah Sultan Husayn in 1706-14 (A.H. 1118-26); the Chahar Bagh (Four Gardens) was the creation of Shah Abbas I. In 1598 (A.H. 1006) he personally supervised the laying out and planting of this processional approach to his capital. A broad canal coursed through the center of the avenue, reflecting the bright flowers and stately sycamores that lined its sides. Between the quiet pools, water splashed down over terraces or sparkled in numerous fountains. Palaces

surrounded by large gardens bordered the street. On ceremonial occasions the paving was covered with brocades, and then a path was spread with sand and strewn with blossoms for the the Shah to ride upon.

TURKEY

The Seljuks evolved new architectural themes on the rugged terrain of eastern Anatolia, as craftsmen in brick turned their skill to structures in stone. Patterns such as those found at Demavand and Kharraqan, feasible in small units of brick, appear rarely in eastern Anatolia, and when they do, they are simplified, as at Eski Malatya. Stone, scarce in Iran, abounds in Turkey. Texture, the fleeting play of light and shadow, becomes the carver's art as stone is chiseled into a fantasy of design.

Different climates pose different problems, especially in the high mountains, where summer is a brief moment between the lashing winter storms. It is said that men's beards freeze in Erzurum; whether or not this is so, shelter is certainly required. The expansive court with its four *iwans* was unsuitable here. Space had to be contained, and protected from piercing winds and sleet. Here, the vaulting of vast interior areas challenged engineering skill.

In Bursa, the early Ottoman capital, there was a brief period of brick and stone construction. Warm textures in rust and pitted gray were the adornment of the Muradiye. Under the Ottomans tile, too, changed. New shades of deep green, orange, and tomato red decorated the walls. Flowers and trees were painted on tiles and became picture-panels in selected areas in the Istanbul mosques. Perhaps this treatment came from the Byzantine use of isolated, rather than structurally oriented, mosaic patterns.

Once they were established in Istanbul, the Ottomans evolved new concepts for religious architecture. Gone were the ornate carved façades of the Seljuks. No longer did tile glisten on the minarets or gleam from the exterior walls. Mosques became compositions in gray stone, with a minimum of ornamentation. Interest had turned to the expression of internal needs in the outward form.

The builders of Iranian mosques, it will be recalled, were not concerned with the exterior effect of an entire building. A great portal, a swelling dome, and tall minarets were regarded as isolated elements, fascinating in themselves and in their relationship to another, nearby, shape. Outer walls tended to vanish into surrounding structures, often becoming simply mud brick, as at Ashtarjan. Even the imposing Shah Mosque in Isfahan has only one exterior view—the magnificent entrance facing the *Maidan*. In Iran the emphasis was on the elevations within the court.

In the work of the Ottoman architect Sinan the difference between Turkey and Iran is readily apparent. In Sinan's buildings all façades are fully developed, and perspectives are taken into account. In addition, exterior forms reveal the interior design. The dome chamber, for example, finds expression in the many cupolas that surround the crowning hemisphere.

The presentation of a group of related buildings in an orderly scheme became an increasing concern of Turkish architects. The Huand Hatun complex (*circa* A.D. 1237; A.H. 635) at Kayseri includes a mosque, a *medrese (madrasa)*, a mausoleum and a bath. The first three of these monuments are grouped together behind a high wall. Within the enclosure, however, the structures are not placed according to any particular design. The Muradiye complex at Bursa (A.D. 1426; A.H. 830) comprises many buildings—mosque, *medrese*, hospital and numerous mausoleums. These are all brick and stone structures of a similar style, and are situated in a small park. The distribution of the buildings is informal, conforming to the slight grades of the site rather than to a rigid plan. The uniformity of the building materials, and the casual paths winding through the garden, give the composition a pleasing unity. The 16th–century Suleymaniye is much greater in scale than the earlier complexes and is designed on an axial plan with the mosque as the focal point.

CHAPTER V **Seljuks of Rum**

(early 12th-late 13th centuries A.D.; early 6th-late 7th centuries A.H.)

The Seljuks presumably were descended from a tribal chief in Turkestan called Seljuk ibn Dukak. This tribe, migrating westward, rapidly conquered most of Iran, and in 1055 a grandson of Seljuk marched into the imperial city of Baghdad. Like a relentless tide, the Turkish invasion flowed still farther west: south into Syria and Palestine; north into Anatolia. For about a hundred years the Seljuk great sultans ruled over an undivided Moslem empire; later their influence declined, and regional sultanates emerged. One of these was the Sultanate of Rum (which comprised Anatolia).

The Arabs called Anatolia *Diyari-Rum* (Land of the Romans), and it is from this title that the name Rum derives. The use of the name Turkey for the Turkish lands in Asia Minor occurs for the first time in 1190 in a chronicle of the crusades. Although Western people adopted this designation, Moslems continued for a long time to call this territory Rum, and one of the 16th–century titles of Suleyman the Magnificent was Sultan of Rum.

Like the Iranians, the Seljuks frequently covered the walls of their buildings with designs. Color (including mosaic tilework) was a major decorative factor with them. Portals became monumental and were elaborately carved, often in high relief.

PLATE 100

ERZURUM. Seljuk tomb tower

This mausoleum *(turbe)* in Erzurum is a Seljuk
tomb tower of the late 12th century
(6th century A.H.). It is located behind the
Cifte Minareli *Medrese*. The stone tomb tower is
decorated on the outside with a casual pattern
in shades of red, gray and white. Gables
surmount the walls of the octagon and form
diagonal lines against the round base of the dome.
The pairs of blind arches are attached to
each other by a plain, linear molding which
outlines them but does not detract from
the simplicity of the façade.

PLATE 101

ERZURUM. Seljuk tomb tower

A stone border joins the cornice of this Seljuk tomb
tower at Erzurum to the outer walls and repeats
the red tones. The stylized head of a ram
seen in this arched window is an integral part
of the exterior design. Its horns stress the curve of
the opening.

PLATE **102**

ERZURUM. Seljuk tomb towers

These Seljuk mausoleums at Erzurum are also
located behind the Cifte Minareli *Medrese*
and probably date from the 13th century
(7th century A.H.). The arcaded cylinder originated
in Erzurum and became the dominant style for
tomb towers in the Van district of Anatolia.
Smaller than the tower illustrated in
Plate 100, the tombs shown here are simple round
structures with pyramidal roofs. Plain moldings
form the arches and create shadows on the
smooth drums. The far tomb has a narrow frieze
of red stone which decorates the space
between the arches and the eaves.

PLATE **103**

ERZURUM. Cifte Minareli *medrese*

This detail is from a column in the courtyard
of the Cifte Minareli *medrese*. The *medrese* is a
stone structure built in Erzurum in 1253 (A.H. 651)
under the patronage of Huand Hatun, the
daughter of a Seljuk prince. The strict Sunni
orthodoxy of the *medrese* (school of
theology) furthered conservatism and unity in the
land. Recognizing this, the government
urged people to build these schools and to adorn
them fittingly. An inscription in the
Cifte Minareli, read by Belin in 1852, reflects this
public-spirited attitude:

" Servants of God! listen to my words because they
are worthy of your attention: In the time of Sultan Melik
Khan, that God eternalize his reign, I left Kharezm
and headed for the country of Rum. When I arrived in
that country I decided to make it my permanent
residence; and in the most fortunate moment the idea
came to me to found an establishment that would always
be a work both pious and meritorious. So I ordered
the construction of this mosque with cells so that the
friends and seekers of knowledge could reside there. I left
to this establishment for necessary repairs, in case of
any destruction, the rental fees from seven shops and
from all the neighboring land on all sides of the
monument. These revenues ... shall be collected and
disbursed annually." [1]

This inscription probably refers to an earlier
building on the same site.

PLATE **104**

ERZURUM. Cifte Minareli *medrese*

A stone column in the courtyard of the
Cifte Minareli *medrese* is decorated with a carved
pattern often seen in Iranian brickwork (Plate 18,
right column, and Plates 19 and 31).

TERCAN. Mama Hatun mausoleum

The Mama Hatun mausoleum *(turbesi)* at Tercan
was built about 1200 (about A.H. 596); the architect
was d'Ebu'n-Nema. The height from the
base is 34 ½ feet (10.5 m.). Rising in simple stone
blocks from a square base with chamfered corners,
the eight curved walls terminate under the
overhang of a steep tent roof.

*Figure K. A Mongol camp, drawing circa
1253, by Friar Rubruquis.*

The Seljuk tent roofs probably derived from the
Mongol tents. Some of these mobile
houses measured 26 feet (8 m.) across, and as
many as twenty-two oxen might be needed to move
them. A rich noble would have as many as
two hundred such vehicles for his wives
and household. These dwellings were felt-lined and
often had luxurious hangings of silks and
brocades. [1]

PLATE 107

ESKI MALATYA. Ulu Cami

This detail of a brick wall is from the sanctuary *iwan* of the Ulu Cami (Masjid-i-Jami) at Eski Malatya. This mosque was built in 1247 (A.H. 645) by Sehabeddin Ilyas, son of Ebubekir, during the reign of Izzuddin Keykavus II, son of Keyhusrev II. The use of white mortar bonding distinguishes this brickwork from Iranian Seljuk styles and gives it a marked individuality. Under the Seljuks of Rum, Malatya was the chief town of the eastern provinces on the Euphrates boundary. Earlier, it was an important Moslem fortress during the wars with Byzantium.[2]

PLATE 108

ESKI MALATYA. Ulu Cami

On the inside of this dome from the Ulu Cami at
Eski Malatya, the swirling patterns of
enameled bricks suggest a singleness of structural
and aesthetic purpose. It is interesting to compare
the decorative treatment of this brick
dome with that of the Sangbast tomb (Plate 2).

PLATE 109

KAYSERI. Sultan *han*

The Sultan *han* (caravanserai) is located thirty-two
miles (fifty kilometers) north of Kayseri on
the Sivas road. The height of this entrance portal to
the main hall is about 51 feet (15.6 m.) and the
overall width is about 30 feet (9 m.). This building
was erected between 1232 and 1236 (*circa* A.H. 650).
Hans were spaced a day's march apart along
the main thoroughfares, where they
served as shelters for travelers. Merchants,
traversing the long roads from east to west, could be
sure of water and security in these compounds
as the custom of the land strictly forbade
attacks on a *han* or robbery within one. The great
caravans were an important source of
revenue and were protected by local governments.
Sometimes a mosque would be included in the
han and, in large cities, a bazaar with baths and
other amenities.

KAYSERI. Sultan *han*

This stone carving on the portal to the main hall of the Sultan *han* is based on a swastika motif.

Figure L. Reconstruction of the Sultan han *near Kayseri, by A. Gabriel.*[1]

On either side of the entrance were apartments for the guardian and personnel of the *han*. In the center of the court shown above is the mosque. The covered hall measures about 152 by 111 feet (approximately 46 by 34 m.). It sheltered animals and men together; this provoked the acid remark from Louis XIV's ambassador, Nointel, that " in a *han*, you hunt for your cook and run into a camel, or when seeking the valet, collide with a mule." [2]

PLATE **111**

KAYSERI. Sultan *han*

This detail of stone carving is on the portal to
the main hall of the Sultan *han*. Seljuk patterns
derived from many sources, such as rugs
and textiles. Stylized forms of plants and animals
(especially snakes), ropes, buttons, and bosses
from harnesses, as well as writing afforded inspiration
for decoration. Often, stars in five-fingered
rosettes were used; this may possibly have
been a survival of the pagan belief in
the five fingers as a talisman against the evil eye.[3]

PLATE **112**

KAYSERI. Sultan *han*

These shafts flank the exterior portal on the
north side of the *han*. The cluster of columns
emerges from a rounded base to form a decorative
bastion for the outer wall.

PLATE **113**

TERCAN. Countryside between Tercan and Tunceli

The mountainous countryside seen here lies
between Tercan and Tunceli. Many people invaded
these Anatolian wilds. Some remained,
others were driven back, but all brought memories
of their past.

What gales of fragrance scent the vernal air!
Hills, dales, and woods, their lovliest mantles wear.
Who knows what cares await that fatal day,
When ruder gusts shall banish gentle May?
Ev'n death, perhaps, our valleys will invade.
Be gay: too soon the flowers of Spring will fade.

Mesihi, " Ode to the Spring " [1]

PLATE **114**

KAYSERI. Cifte *medrese*

This detail is from the entrance to the eastern *medrese* of the Cifte *medrese* at Kayseri. The western *medrese* (*cifte* means pair) bears the inscribed date A.H. 602; probably both were erected between 1205 and 1212 (A.H. 601-607), during the reign of Giyasuddin Keyhusrev I.[1] This *medrese* was one of the earliest Seljuk monuments in Kayseri; the structure is in a simple style throughout, and has fine proportions. Diez has stated: " The impression of strength created by the strong lines of relief moldings and cornices is a result of shadows—shadows that reach beyond to create monumentality."[2]

Kayseri, known in Roman times as Caesarea, was the second town of Rum. Well situated on a major trade route, Kayseri has been an important city for many centuries. Mustawfi visited it in 1340 (A.H. 740), and described it as a large town surrounded by high stone walls.[3]

PLATE 115

KAYSERI. Huand Hatun mausoleum

The Huand Hatun mausoleum (Khuand Turbesi)
at Kayseri was built about 1237-38 (about
A.H. 635) by Princess Mahperi, wife of Keykubad I.
The octagonal tomb, which is 28 feet (9.6 m.)
in diameter, was the last structure erected
in a complex which included a bath, a mosque, and
a *medrese*. A tracery of fine patterns is carved on the
stone walls and the corner colonnettes. The
cornice is rounded at each end to form capitals for
the shafts. Stalactites enliven the marble base.

PLATE 116

NIGDE. Sunghur Bey Mosque

The Sunghur Bey Mosque at Nigde was built about
1335-36 (about A.H. 736), under the patronage
of Sunghur Agra, a Mongol chieftain. This forbidding
north façade is scaled down to a human size
through the use of a small doorway and
a horizontal molding; the latter, which partly
encloses the doorway, breaks up the height of the
wall. A blending of Moslem and Christian
styles is evident throughout the monument; for
instance, on this elevation a rose window
is introduced. These foreign innovations may be
attributed to the presence of laborers
imported from other areas. [1] This evokes speculation
as to the architectural procedures involved in
Seljuk construction. It would appear that at least
the decorative treatment of the monuments
usually followed the traditional motifs of the
craftsmen rather than a preconceived plan.

PLATE **117**

KONYA. Karatay *medrese*

This detail of a corner is from the Karatay *medrese* a t Konya, which was built 1251-52 (A.H. 650) by the order of the Emir Celaluddin Karatay, a vizier of Keykavus II.· According to Diez, the walls were originally completely tiled.[1] The transition from a square chamber to a dome is achieved here by a device quite different from the Iranian squinch. The dome rests on four flattened pendentives (sometimes called Turkish triangles) located at the corners of the square chamber, and also on the four midpoints of the walls. Each pendentive is composed of five inverted triangles. The bases of these inverted triangles support the drum; their apexes transfer the weight of the dome to the corners of the building.

Konya (ancient Iconium) was the capital of the Seljuks of Rum from the beginning of the 12th to the end of the 13th centuries, when the Mongol invasions ended the Seljuk rule. At the height of her importance, Konya was said to have as many *medreses* as Baghdad.

KONYA. Karatay *medrese*

The complex pattern seen in this detail of a tile
panel in the Karatay *medrese*, is based on
interlocking parallelograms which are placed at
various angles to each other. As has been illustrated
(Kharraqan towers, Plates 17-26), Seljuk
artists were masters at camouflaging basic geometric
shapes in complicated designs. The high relief
of this particular panel is accentuated by
the color and the gleaming surfaces of the tiles.
Extensive use of stone and deeply incised carving
probably contributed to the interest of the Seljuks
of Rum in high-relief tilework.

KONYA. Sircali *medrese*

These examples are from the Sircali *medrese* at
Konya, which was built in 1243 (A.H. 644), during
the reign of Keyhusrev II. Aubergine is combined
with light blue on the façade of the main
iwan. Within the *iwan*, a deeper turquoise is
patterned with black enamel bricks.

The Mongol invasions were a powerful catalyst in
the diffusion of artistic concepts, as the
conquerors conscripted craftsmen for work in their
cities and many other artists emigrated to evade
the attacks. Deeply devoted to the beautification
of his capital, Konya, Keyhusrev summoned
learned men and artists from Isfahan, whence
many had fled to escape the Mongol raids.
An inscription on the frieze of the Sircali *medrese*
attributes the work to an Iranian builder.
It reads: " The work of Muhammad ibn
Muhammad ibn Osman, al-banna, of Tus." In all
the towns of Asia Minor, talented Iranians
were active during the Seljuk rule. An especially
interesting point in the relationship between the
two countries is that true mosaic faience
occurred first in Turkey. The art of creating an
almost completely glazed surface may have traveled
west with Iranian artisans, but the delicate,
closely fitted patterns in glazed tiles of various
colors seen in the Karatay *medrese* (Plates 117 and
118) precede the earliest known examples of
mosaic faience in Iran by about fifty years.[1]

CHAPTER VI

Ottomans: Bursa Period

(circa A.D. 1300-1453; *circa* A.H. 699-857)

In 1326 (A.H. 726) Bursa was captured by Orhan and became the first Ottoman capital. Orhan was the son of Osman, tribal chief of the Osmanlis. It was this tribal name which Europeans corrupted to "Ottomans." Seven years after the conquest, Ibn Battuta visited Bursa and commented on the well laid out town with its wide streets.[1] Several religious monuments were built in the 14th century, but in 1402 (A.H. 805) Timur captured the city, and the following decade was a period of internecine strife. The reestablishment of a strong Ottoman government under Mehmet I (A.D. 1413-21; A.H. 816-24) brought renewed prosperity to the capital, and several fine buildings date from his reign and that of his son, Murad II (1421-51). The seat of government was moved to Istanbul shortly after 1453 (A.H. 857), but Pierre Belon, visiting in the mid-16th century, reported that "Bursa is more populated and richer than Istanbul."[2] The city's wealth came mainly from trade and from silk manufacture.

The Bursa School of Ottoman architecture was a continuation of the Seljuk style rather than the forerunner of the 16th-century mosques in Istanbul. This was true both structurally and decoratively. The stability of the dome continued to be assured by heavy walls. The zone of transition was still accomplished through triangular surfaces (whereas in the later period the true pendentive was used). Fenestration was not yet a major concern. The treatment of a vast inner space and its exterior expression received little consideration. There were certain changes, however. The coordinated dome was an innovation of the Bursa School. Also, the importance of the portal decreased at this time. In Seljuk monuments the entrance dominates the façade, whereas at Bursa the former is frequently hidden behind an arcaded porch. This architectural feature may have been adopted from the Byzantines, but it was the Ottomans who developed it. As Ottoman style matured under Sinan in the 16th century, the coordinated dome and the diminished role of the entrance portal became important factors in the creation of a harmonious entity for all the elements of a building.

Both the design and the execution of early Ottoman faience at Bursa show a marked continuity with the Seljuk work at Konya. The composition of the clay is also very similar. Chemical analysis proves that the same metallic bases were employed in the glazes—cobalt for deep blue, antimony for yellow, manganese for black, tin for white and derivatives of copper for green and turquoise. The earlier Seljuk designs of arabesques, geometric patterns and stylized floral motifs continued to be used in most Bursa ceramic decoration.

PLATE **121**

BURSA. Green Turbe

The Green Mausoleum (Yesil Turbe) at Bursa is the
tomb of Mehmet I. It was built from 1413 to 1421
(A.H. 816-24), under the patronage of Haci Iwad,
Governor of Bursa, but the decoration was
probably not completed until 1424 (A.H. 827).
It is an octagonal structure on a stone base, trimmed
in white marble, and covered by a dome.
Originally the roof was faced with green tiles
probably glazed, but it now has a lead covering. The
building measures about 88 feet (27 m.) in
height and about 68 feet (21 m.) in diameter.
Its color—a lovely turquoise shimmering through the
dark cedars—is the glory of this monument.

PLATE **122**

BURSA. Green Turbe

This pattern is from a panel on the exterior of the *qibla* wall of the Green Turbe at Bursa. As a concept of the early 15th century, this abstract design is interesting and provocative.

PLATE **123**

BURSA. Green Turbe

The *mihrab* of the Green Turbe in Bursa is shown
here. André Godard believes that the idea of
facing the mihrab toward Mecca came from the
Christian orientation of the apse of the
basilica. He offers the following conjecture. In the
early 7th century no particular need was felt
for religious buildings, as the Prophet had said
that all places of prayer were equal in the
eyes of God. In fact *masjid*, which is translated as
mosque, means simply a place of prostration.
The growing number of converts, however,
required for prestige reasons a dignified setting for
congregational worship. This desire for suitable
buildings led to the appropriation of Byzantine
Christian churches. Adopting the symbolism of the
apse but turning the apse into a *qibla* wall with a
mihrab directed toward Mecca, was a quick and
dramatic method of adjustment.[1]

PLATE **124**

BURSA. Green Turbe

The carved stucco (even the gold tracery) is submerged beneath the astounding intensity of the colors in this doorway in the Green Turbe.

The original, wooden doors carried the inscription: " Work of Ali b. Hajji Ahmad of Tabriz." It is probable that, as decorator and ceramist, he also contributed to the construction and embellishment of the tomb.[2]

PLATE **125**

BURSA. Muradiye Mosque

The west view of the mosque in the Muradiye
complex at Bursa is seen here. Construction,
completed in 1426 (A.H. 830) was under the
patronage of Murad II. The Muradiye group
includes a mosque and a *medrese,* as well as several
mausoleums; all the buildings are arranged
informally in a garden and are placed so as to
harmonize with the gentle slopes of the terrain. The
outer walls of the mosque are faced with stone
and brick courses; the domes, though now
covered with lead, were originally tiled.

PLATE **126**

BURSA. Muradiye *medrese*

The north wall of the study area in the *medrese*
of the Muradiye complex, Bursa, is shown.
The height to the top of the cornice is 36 feet
(11 m.), and the arch measures about 20 feet
(approximately 6 m.) in height and about 24 feet
(approximately 7.25 m.) in width. The proportions
of the dome roof can be seen in Figure M.

*Figure M. North elevation of the medrese in the
Muradiye complex, drawing by A. Gabriel.*

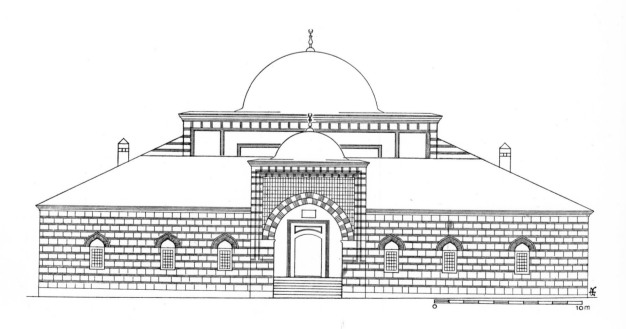

PLATE **127** BURSA. Detail of plate 126

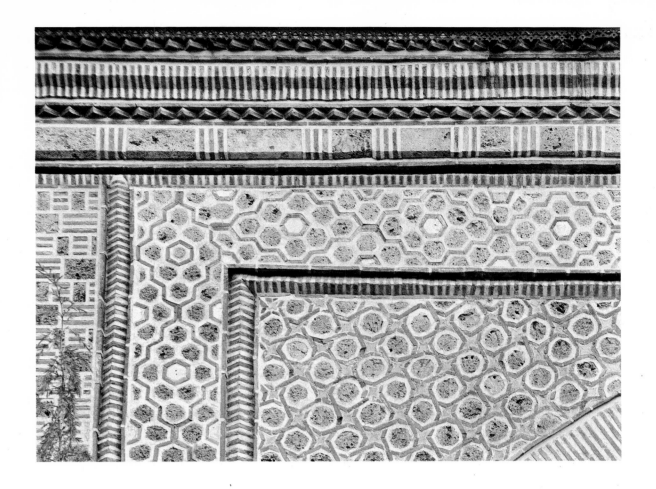

PLATE **128**

BURSA. Muradiye *medrese*

This detail is from the exterior wall of the
Muradiye *medrese.* The rough shape and texture of
the stone contrast with the smooth man-made
forms of the brick. The combination of brick and
stone occurs frequently in Byzantine walls, and
there was undoubtedly some Byzantine influence
in the Ottoman style. Far more significant factors,
however, were the convenience of the materials,
the relative Ottoman poverty in the 15th century
and the desire for rapid completion of the
monuments. Clay was locally available, as was
wood for firing the kilns. Marble and
dressed stone were expensive at a time when
the treasury was strained by recent wars and
preparations for new campaigns. The Muradiye
mosque and *medrese* were built in eighteen
months—a feat scarcely possible with marble and
stone.

CHAPTER VII

**Ottomans:
Istanbul
Periods**

(A.D. 1453-1922; A.H. 857-1340)

Ottoman architecture after the conquest of Constantinople in 1453 was quite different from the earlier Bursa style. The overall composition of a complex of buildings, or of an individual monument, became the primary aesthetic consideration. Structures were oriented on axial plans with all perspectives taken into account. Each architectural element contributed to the total effect, but no single one predominated overwhelmingly, as did the Seljuk entrance portal. Ornamentation, such as elaborate carving, was now minimized and exterior tilework eliminated. Faience inside buildings became purely decorative with no relation to structure. Tile panels themselves became pictorial; more colors were used, and detail grew more intricate.

The study of the source of styles is interesting, but the issue can be overstressed, as has certainly been the case with Ottoman art. As Professor Berenson said, " Influences count for little where there is no genius to be affected." [1] The Turkish architect Koca Sinan was a genius, and his designs are far from being mere imitations of Byzantine plans.

Sancta Sophia undoubtedly served as a challenge to the Ottoman artist's imagination and evoked in him a desire to create monuments of equal magnificence. The domed chamber was by this time a traditional solution for the builders of mosques, as it was fundamentally better adapted to Moslem devotional needs than was a Hellenistic columned hall. But even the vast interior of Sancta Sophia was not entirely suitable for Moslem ritual. The Christian service involves processional rituals, and an axial plan of considerable depth is desirable. This is not the case with Moslem services, where prayer is led from one position and the congregation participates in the obeisances. For this, a shallow rectangle with an uninterrupted radial view is the most advantageous plan. Ottoman architects were constantly seeking a satisfactory design for an interior, a design entirely suitable to their particular needs. In this search Sancta Sophia may best be considered an original impetus; a marked evolution can be noted in the Sokullu Mehmet Pasha Mosque, Istanbul (Figure N).

A significant departure from this Byzantine monument is also evident in the external appearance of Istanbul mosques during and after the time of Sinan. A lighter and far more coordinated structure has emerged. The central dome and the supporting half-domes are more vertical—an innovation dictated by aesthetic rather than strictly technical exigencies. The domed elements achieve a compact expression, in which each part contributes visually to the composition. Buttresses and other features which give Sancta Sophia a confusing outline are placed nearer the corners and are assimilated into the overall plan of the rising cupolas. Broad arches break the monotony of these bulbous domes and create a new rhythm within a compatible whole. Finally, fenestration is no longer merely a means of interior lighting but is appreciated as a decorative adjunct to the façades and as a method of reducing the ponderous appearance of the buildings.

PLATE **129**

ISTANBUL. Rustem Pasha Mosque

The detail shown here is from a panel on the outside of the northwest wall of the Rustem Pasha Mosque in Istanbul. The mosque was built in 1564 (A.H. 971) by Koca Sinan, for the Grand Vizier Rustem Pasha. Painted tiles have replaced the mosaic work of the Seljuks, and the color range has been increased to include more shades of blue, green, rust and red. The colors were vitrifiable pastes which were covered with a transparent glaze. A marked decrease in stylization can be seen in this panel. Although the design remains linear and there is no attempt at perspective, an awareness of the natural beauty of flowers in full bloom is evident. In aesthetic interpretation they approach in feeling Chinese and Japanese flower paintings. Unlike the Oriental artists, however, with their predilection for simplicity and sparseness, the Turkish designers usually depicted the luxuriantly abundant, almost wasteful, profusion of Nature.

PLATE **130**

ISTANBUL. Rustem Pasha Mosque

This panel, with its graceful design, is from the outside of the northwest wall of the Rustem Pasha Mosque. Tiles for the important Ottoman mosques were designed in Istanbul by artists working under the supervision of a " Director of Faience," and were then dispatched to Iznik (ancient Nicaea) for execution. Three to four hundred tile factories and pottery kilns were located in Iznik in the 16th century, despite the fact that all materials, including wood for firing the kilns, had to be imported. Iznik tiles were usually 9½ inches (24 cm.) square by ¾ to 1¼ inches (2-3 cm.) thick.[1] They were cut in a slightly conical shape to ensure a tight fit. The most brilliant color that appears in Ottoman tilework is bolus red. This vibrant shade was in use only from the mid-16th to the mid-17th centuries. The raw material for this color, an iron oxide clay silicate which does not fuse with the alkaline glaze, was obtained from the neighborhood of Kutahya; another, more yellow, variety came from Armenia.

A. J. Butler, in his book *Islamic Pottery*, states that bolus red in a relief type of application has been excavated at Tell el-Amarna, Egypt, in work dating from the Akhnaten period in the 14th century B.C. It is also seen in the Raqqa ware of Syria, which dates from the 12th century A.D., and, in Istanbul, in Byzantine household pottery of the 10th and 11th centuries A.D. [2]

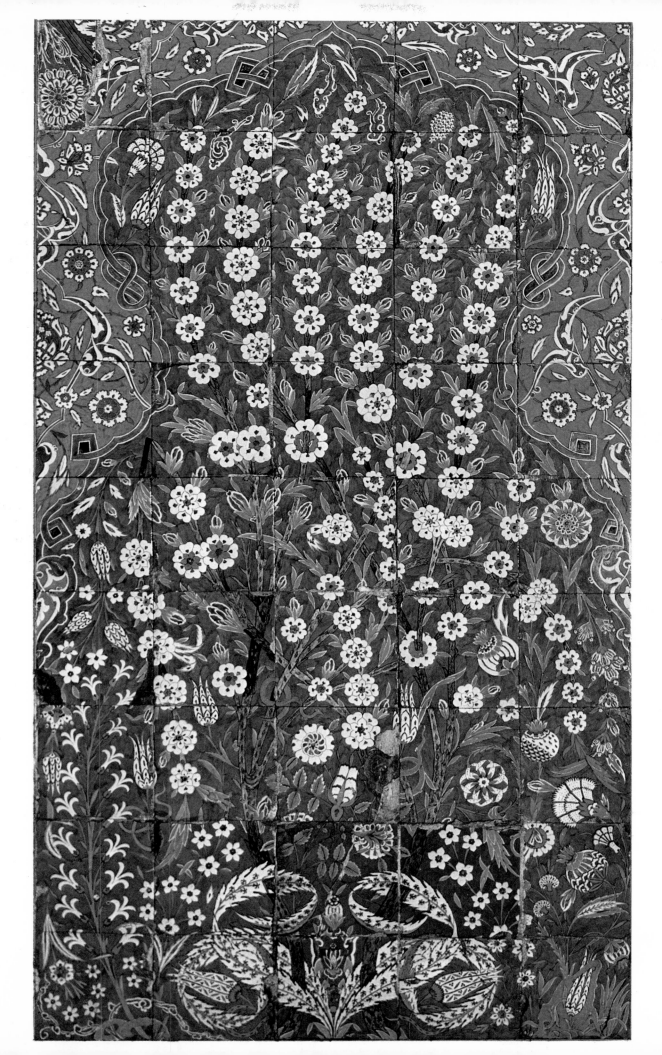

PLATE **131**

ISTANBUL. Rustem Pasha Mosque

The flowers on this panel at the head of the
minbar in the Rustem Pasha Mosque look fresh and
lively despite the symmetry of the design.
Characteristically, the bolus red appears as a
glowing accent in the center of the blossoms.
Rustem Pasha was Vizier to Suleyman the
Magnificent.

PLATE **132**

ISTANBUL. Mihrimah Mosque

This view shows the northwest side of the
Mihrimah Mosque in Istanbul, built in 1540 or 1555
(A.H. 947 or 962) as a memorial to Princess
Mihrimah, daughter of Suleyman and wife of
Rustem Pasha. The genius of the architect,
Koca Sinan, can be seen in such features as the
fenestration, the sloping buttresses encircling the
dome, and the sophisticated balance of the
composition as a whole. A single minaret darts
skyward, its narrow silhouette in dramatic contrast
to the mass of the mosque.

PLATE **133**   ISTANBUL. Sokullu Mehmet Pasha Mosque

Figure N. Plan of the Sokullu Mehmet Pasha Mosque, Istanbul.

The dome of the Sokullu Mehmet Pasha Mosque in Istanbul surmounts six great arches. This monument was built in 1571-72 (A.H. 979) for Sokullu Mehmet, Grand Vizier and son-in-law of Selim II. In the design of this mosque, Sinan eliminated all internal structural divisions.

A hexagon forms the transition from a rectangular chamber to a circular dome; two sides and four corners of the hexagon are placed on the long walls of the rectangle. In the center of the short walls two massive piers jut out: these support the fifth and sixth corners. Four sides of the hexagon rest on arches which spring from these piers and the long sides of the rectangle, traversing the corners. The transition from this six-sided shape to the circular base of the dome is achieved through the use of six spherical pendentives. Four half-domes roof the four corners of the structure.

Two low balconies, which are not part of the basic structural design, appear in the plan as dotted lines forming an almost square rectangle. The painted decoration is 19th century.

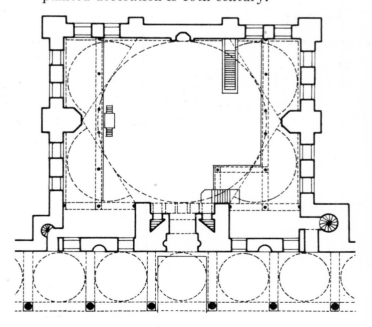

PLATE **134**

ISTANBUL. Sokullu Mehmet Pasha Mosque

This tile panel is to the left of the *minbar* in the
Sokullu Mehmet Pasha Mosque. The *minbar*
is adorned with marble and gilt decoration. The
complexity of the tile pattern on the panel disguises
its frequent repeats.

Koca Sinan, designer of the mosque, was born
near Kayseri in 1490. His education at the Palace
School was terminated in the military division, and
he became an engineer in the Janissaries. Here
he was commissioned to build bridges and other
military structures, but he did not begin his
career in civil architecture until he was forty-seven
years old. According to his memoirs, in the next
fifty-one years he designed 312 monuments.
He became Chief Architect to the Palace in 1539,
and his fame soon spread to other countries. At the
request of the Moghul Emperor of India, he sent
some of his architects to assist in the design of
the buildings of Agra.

PLATE **135**

ISTANBUL. Suleymaniye

A stately entrance frames the approach to the forecourt of the Suleymaniye (Mosque of Suleyman) in Istanbul, built in 1550-57 (A.H. 957-64). Ornament here is at a minimum and serves mostly to accentuate the vertical nature of this façade. Tall, narrow engaged columns are seen at the corners of the building, on the inner side of the doorway and, with greater prominence, flanking the portal and extending upward, so as to divide the wall. A more important device for the partitioning of space is the use of dark openings—simple rectangles in the windows and a deeper recess in the doorway. Sinan, who designed the building, had visited Italy for a short time, and the character of this façade suggests the Italian Renaissance.

The Suleymaniye complex occupies an area 975 by 1140 feet (about 296 by 347 m.) square. The schools, hospital, bathhouse, library, almshouse and other buildings are placed on rectangular sites whose lines parallel those of the mosque, which is the focal monument of the plan. The orderly design of the complex and the intricate structure of the mosque itself, make it difficult to believe that Sinan worked without scaled plans. No such drawings have been found, however. Those contemporary plans that we have are never scale drawings but are merely sketches with measurements given in figures. C. E. Arseven feels that the architect gave the master artisan the proportions and measurements of the parts to be built and indicated the type of decoration to be used. The craftsmen would then submit their ideas, derived from traditional models, to the architect.[1] It is known that Sinan worked closely with his builders and was intimately concerned with every detail of the work. His vast output, however, would almost preclude the possibility that personal supervision replaced detailed drawings.

PLATE **136**

ISTANBUL. Sultan Ahmet Mosque

The panel shown here is in the north gallery of the
Sultan Ahmet Mosque, often called the
Blue Mosque, in Istanbul. This monument was
built 1609-16 (A.H. 1018-25), under the patronage of
Sultan Ahmet I, by his chief architect,
Mohammed Aga.

Vines twine gracefully about a severely geometric
cypress in this 17th-century panel. Although the
leaves are drawn with botanical precision and
the texture of the trunk of the tree is indicated,
it is the abstract treatment (common in this later
period) of color and line which strikes the viewer.
The natural charm of a plant has been suppressed
in stylized motifs.

The cypress was a symbol of eternal life. In
Ottoman designs it is frequently entwined with an
arabesque of grapevines.

PLATE **137**

ISTANBUL. Sultan Ahmet Mosque

The panel seen here is from the north gallery
of the Sultan Ahmet Mosque. The culture of tulips
became a passion of the Ottoman court as early
as the first half of the 16th century; it reached
its peak two hundred years later. Busbeck,
the horticulturist who imported tulips, lilacs and
hyacinths into Europe, wrote the following
in 1554: " Turks cultivate flowers with great care
and do not hesitate to spend for a particularly
beautiful blossom a considerable sum, though
otherwise they are a thrifty people." He also stated
that flowers were spread in the mosques " in such
quantities that the worshipers could barely leave
the edifice." [1]

PLATE **138**

ISTANBUL. Sultan Ahmet Mosque

Originally, the Sultan Ahmet Mosque (seen here from the north) was part of a complex.

The soaring minarets counterbalancing the mass of the building, the smaller cupolas rising wave upon wave to the summation of the dome—these are the mosques of Istanbul.

Glossary

Cami In Turkey, the congregational mosque.

Han A Turkish term; called a caravanserai in Afghanistan and Iran, the *han* is a place of shelter for travelers; usually has an open courtyard which is surrounded by covered arcades.

Hegira The flight of Muhammad from Mecca to Medina in A.D. 622. The Moslems date their era from then onward, so that A.D. 622=A.H. 1. Hegira years are lunar, and consist of twelve lunar months. These years retrogress through all the seasons every 32½ years.

Iwan A vaulted portal or hall open to the exterior and framed by a great arch. The form was taken over by Islamic builders in Iran from earlier Sassanian structures.

Jami or Masjid-i-Jami In Iran and Afghanistan, the congregational or Friday mosque.

Khanaqah A monastery.

Madrasa A school of theology or secondary school, covering a wider educational field than the strictly religious.

Maidan A town square or plaza.

Masjid A mosque; the literal translation is ' the place where one throws oneself on the ground ' (place of prostration).

Medrese The Turkish term for a *madrasa*.

Mihrab The prayer niche marking the direction of Mecca, to which all Moslem prayers are addressed. The main *mihrab* is usually the focal point of structure and decoration.

Minaret	A shaft adjoining or connected to a Moslem religious building. From the minaret the call to prayer was made five times a day. Some of the tall later minarets were difficult to climb and were purely for decorative purposes. Poetically, minarets signify the rising of the believer's prayers.
Minbar	The pulpit, or stairway and platform from which passages from the Koran are read on Friday.
Musalla	A structure serving as a place of prayer, and generally located outside the city walls.
Pendentive	A spherical triangle of masonry, rising from the angles of a square or polygonal base. It effects the transition from the base to a circular dome.
Qibla	Wall directed toward Mecca, and against which a *mihrab*, if one is used, would be placed. Early Moslem religious centers sometimes had only a *qibla* wall and no *mihrab*.
Shia	A large group of diverse Islamic sects which recognize Ali, the son-in-law of Muhammad, and his descendants as the spiritual inheritors of the Prophet. Most Iranians are Shi'ites.
Squinch	An arch which traverses a corner diagonally, and which gives intermediary support to a circular or octagonal dome. Through the use of squinches, a square space may be converted to an octagon, and then, if desired, to a sixteen-sided polygon; upon either of these, a dome is easily constructed. The open space between the arch and the corners bridged may be treated with quarter vaults or with stalactites.
Stalactites	Non-structural, three-dimensional forms used to decorate and fill spaces beneath arches and squinches, and on cornices. They are also called *muqarna* and honeycombs.
Sufism	The doctrine of the Islamic mystics.
Sunni	The orthodox branch of Islam. Turkish Moslems are mainly Sunnis.
Talar	An open porch with columns, attached to a house or palace.
Turbe	In Turkey, a mausoleum.
Zone of Transition	The area in which a square or polygonal base is transformed into a circular shape.

Chronology

IRAN

Seljuks (1037-1194). Descendants of Seljuk, a chieftain from Turkestan.

Il-Khanids (1256-*circa* 1340). Mongols, descendants of Genghis Khan.

Timurids (1380-1499). Descendants of Timur, from Turkestan.

Safavids (1499-1736). Iranian dynasty (having Turkish ancestry).

TURKEY

Seljuks of Rum (early 12th-late 13th centuries). Descendants of Seljuk, a chieftain from Turkestan.

Ottomans (*circa* 1300-1922). Descendants of Osman, Turkish chieftain of a principality in northeastern Turkey.

Bibliographical Notes

Full entries for the reference works cited in these notes will be found in the Bibliography on page 309. Abbreviated titles which are used here appear in the Bibliography in brackets preceding the full title.

Plate 1, Tomb Tower of Kabus, Gurgan

Godard, in *Survey*, III, p. 972.
Omar Khayyam, *Rubaiyat*, p. 79.
Byron, *Road to Oxiana*, pp. 227–32; Godard, *Art of Iran*, p. 300 (for plan); Kai Ka'us ibn Iskandar, *Qabus Nama* (The author was a grandson of Kabus ibn Washmgir and gives an interpretation of social customs, morals and outlook of the period.); Pope, *Persian Architecture*, pp. 86, 95; *Survey*, III, pp. 970–74 (for technical description), 985–86.

Plates 2-3, Tomb of Arslan Jadhib, Sangbast

Schroeder, in *Survey*, III, p. 987.
Athar-é Iran, IV, pp. 10, 14, 264, 295; Diez, *Churanische Baudenkmäler*, pp. 52–56, Plates XIV-XVIII; Pope, *Persian Architecture*, pp. 95, 99–100; *Survey*, III, pp. 986–88, 1275–77.

Plates 4-8, Seljuk Period Tomb Tower, Demavand

Le Strange, *Eastern Caliphate*, p. 371; Lutyens, " Persian Brickwork, II, " *Country Life*, LXXIII (February 4, 1933), pp. 118–23; Morier, *Second Journey*, p. 354, Plate XV; Pope, " Persian Brickwork, " *Country Life*, LXXII (December 31, 1932), pp. 742–47; Stronach and Young, " Three Seljuk Tomb Towers," *Iran*, IV (1966), pp. 1–6, 16–20, Figures 2–4, Plates I–VI; Stuart, *Journal*, p. 249; *Survey*, III, pp. 1035–43 (on early Iranian brickwork); Wilber, *Islamic Iran*, pp. 47–51, 131.

Plates 9-16, Masjid-i-Jami, Isfahan

Nassiri Khosrau, *Relation du voyage*, pp. 252-53.
Conversations with the author.
Some scholars dispute this date and place the vaults in a period prior to the Seljuk. Godard attributes them to a later period, the Muzaffarid (1340-90).
[4] Godard, in *Athar-é Iran*, I, p. 226.
[5] For Herzfeld plan see *Survey*, III, pp. 954-55.
Ars Islamica, II, pp. 7–44; *Athar-é Iran*, I, pp. 213–82; *ibid.*, II, pp. 20-26; *ibid.*, IV, p. 363; Byron, *Road to Oxiana*, pp. 196-97; Chardin, *Voyages*, VIII, pp. 1–10; Coste, *Monuments modernes*; p. 21, Plates IV–V; Dieulafoy, *Perse*, p. 158; Diez, *D.K.d. islamischen Völker*, I, p. 108; *Encyclopedia of World Art*, XII, pp. 863–71; Le Strange, *Eastern Caliphate*, pp. 203–05; Pope, *North Dome*; Pope, *Persian Architecture*, p. 107; Sarre, *Denkmäler*, p. 75; *Survey*, III, pp. 1004–09, 1029–35.

Plates 17-26, Two Seljuk Period Tomb Towers, Kharraqan

[1] Drawing after Jacobstahl, from Sarre, *Denkmäler*, pp. 10-11.
Stern, " Inscriptions "; Stronach and Young, " 11th-Century Seljuk Tombs Discovered in Western Iran," *Illustrated London News* (September 25, 1965), pp. 38–39; Stronach and Young, " Three Seljuk Tomb Towers," *Iran*, IV (1966), pp. 6–20.
General period and brickwork references are as follows: *Encyclopedia of World Art*, XII, pp. 863–71; Lutyens, " Persian Brickwork, II "; Pope, " Persian Brickwork "; *Survey*, III, pp. 1035–43; Wilber, *Islamic Iran*, pp. 47–51.

Plate 27, Courtyard in Masjid-i-Jami, Nayin

[1] *Athar-é Iran*, I, pp. 190-91 (for plan of mosque and illustration of stucco); *Survey*, VIII, pp. 265-69.
Ars Islamica, V, pp. 21–28; *Athar-é Iran*, I, pp. 185-213; Pope, *Persian Architecture*, p. 85; *Survey*, III, p. 935; Flury, " La mosquée de Nayin, " *Syria*, XI, pp. 43-58.

Plates 30-36, Tomb Towers of Surkh and Kabud, Maragha

[1] According to Eric Schroeder (*Survey*, III, p. 1025), probably eight different molds were used to create the brick shapes for the Gunbad-i-Surkh.

[2] The Gunbad-i-Kabud is often presumed to be the tomb of Hulagu's mother, but, as Godard points out, that is, for chronological reasons, quite impossible (*Athar-é Iran*, I, p. 142).

Athar-é Iran, I, pp. 125–60; Godard, *Art of Iran*, pp. 299-306; Pope, *Persian Architecture*, p. 95; Sarre, *Denkmäler*, p. 16; Godard, *Les monuments de Maragha*, pp. 6–11; *Survey*, III, pp. 1024-25, 1042.

Chapter II, Il-Khanid Period

[1] Rashid ad-Din, Letter 51, as quoted in Wilber, *Islamic Iran*, pp. 20–21.

Plate 37; Figure E, Mosque of Ali Shah (The Arg), Tabriz

[1] Taj'ad-Din Ali Shah's name appears three times in the painted ornament of the Oljeitu mausoleum in Sultaniya, which leads Dr. Pope to suggest that he may have been the architect of that tomb (Pope, *Persian Architecture*, note 161).

[2] *Travels to Tana and Persia*; "Travels of a Merchant in Persia," p. 167.

Battuta, *Voyages*, II, pp. 129-30; Chardin, *Voyages*, I, pp. 255-57; Curzon, *Persian Question*, I, p. 522; Dieulafoy, *Perse*, p. 52; Flandin, *Relation du voyage*, I, 176-77; Hookham, *Tamerlaine*, pp. 101-02; Jackson, *Persia*, pp. 40-46; Ker Porter, *Travels*, I, p. 222; Lamb, *Tamerlane*, pp. 293-97; Le Strange, *Eastern Caliphate*, pp. 159-62; Lockhart, *Famous Cities*, pp. 19–25; Pope, *Persian Architecture*, pp. 177–79; *Survey*, III, pp. 1056-61; *Travels to Tana and Persia*, pp. 166–78; Wilber, *Islamic Iran*, pp. 24–25, 146–49.

Figure F; Plates 38-46, Mausoleum of Oljeitu Khudabanda, Sultaniya

[1] Clavijo, *Embassy*, pp. 158-62.

[2] Godard, in *Survey*, III, p. 115.

[3] Godard feels that this ornamentation is of a much later date than the building itself, but other scholars believe it to be either contemporary with or nearly contemporary with the building.

[4] Wilber, *Islamic Iran*, p. 44, Plate LXXXII.

[5] *Ibid.*, p. 44.

Athar-é Iran, IV, pp. 321-22; Byron, *Road to Oxiana*, pp. 50-51; Chardin, *Voyages* II, p. 376; Clavijo, *op. cit.*, p. 153; Contarini, in *Travels to Tana and Persia*, pp. 128–29; M. Dieulafoy, *L'art antique*, p. 172; *Encyclopedia of World Art*, VII, pp. 788-98; Flandin, *Relation du voyage*, I, pp. 202–04; Flandin and Coste, *Voyage*, Plates XI–XII; Godard, *Art of Iran*, pp. 293, 306–12; Ker Porter, *Travels*, I, pp. 275-80; Le Strange, *Eastern Caliphate*, pp. 5, 10, 222, 228–29; Olearius, *Muskowitische*, p. 479; Pope, *Persian Architecture*, p. 172; Sarre, *Denkmäler*, p. 16; *Survey*, III, pp. 1062–63, 1103–18; Tavernier,

Les six voyages, p. 73; Texier, *Description de l'Arméni* II, p. 76; Wilber, *Islamic Iran*, pp. 23–25, 38, 102, 139–4

Plate 47, Mausoleum of Chelebi Oglu, Sultaniya

[1] Some scholars date this monument 1330–33 (A.F 730–733).

Dieulafoy, *Perse*, p. 92; *Encyclopedia of World Art*, VI pp. 788-98; Flandin, *Relation du voyage*, I, p. 20! Flandin and Coste, *Voyage*, Plate X; Sarre, *Denkmäle* pp. 22–23; *Survey*, III, p. 1099; Wilber, *Islamic Ira* pp. 103, 175.

Plates 48-49, Sanctuary of Bayazid Bistami; Masjid-Jami, Bistam

Athar-é Iran, I, p. 60; Curzon, *Persian Question*, pp. 283-85; Fraser, *Narrative of a Journey*, p. 34(Godard, *Art of Iran*, pp. 310-11; Herzfeld, "Reise bericht," *Zeitschrift der deutschen morgenländische Gesellschaft*, V (1926), 3, p. 278; Le Strange, *Easter Caliphate*, pp. 365–66; Pope, *Persian Architectur* p. 150; Sarre, *Denkmäler*, pp. 116–19; *Survey*, II pp. 1081–86, 1293–1320 (the latter for discussion « stucco ornamentation); Wilber, *Islamic Iran*, pp. 79–8 (for discussion of stucco ornamentation), 127–28.

Plate 50, Mausoleum of Pir-i-Bakran, Linjan

Athar-é Iran, II, pp. 29-35; Herzfeld, *Archaeologicc History*, p. 106; Herzfeld, "Reisebericht," *Zeitschri der deutschen morgenländischen Gesellschaft*, V (1926 p. 278; Bahrami, "Some Examples of Il-Khanid Art, pp. 257-60; Pope, *Persian Architecture*, p. 183; *Surve* III, pp. 1077-79; Wilber, *Islamic Iran*, pp. 121-24.

Plates 51-53, Village View; Masjid-i-Jami, Ashtarjan

Smith and Smith, "Islamic Monuments," pp. 213-16 *Survey*, III, pp. 1079-80; Wilber, *Islamic Iran*, pp. 141-44

Plates 54-56, Khanaqah; Mausoleum of Shaykh Al al-Samad al-Isfahani, Natanz

[1] Pope, *Persian Architecture*, p. 179.

Ars Islamica, IX, pp. 37-40, 211–17; *Athar-é Iran*, pp. 83–102; Dieulafoy, *Perse*, pp. 111–12; Pop« *Persian Architecture*, pp. 179-83; *Survey*, III, pp. 1086 89; Wilber, *Islamic Iran*, pp. 133–34.

Plates 57-58, Masjid-i-Jami, Varamin

Ars Islamica, II, pp. 134-35; *Athar-é Iran*, IV, 309-22 Byron, *Road to Oxiana*, p. 48; Herzfeld, "Reisebericht, *Zeitschrift der deutschen morgenländischen Gesellschaft*, (1926), 3, p. 234; Minorsky, "The Mosque of Varamin, pp. 155-58; Pope, *Persian Architecture*, p. 183; Sarr« *Denkmäler*, pp. 59-64; *Survey*, III, pp. 1093-96; Wilbe *Islamic Iran*, pp. 158-59.

Chapter III, **Timurid Period**; Plate 59, **Husein Bayqara Madrasa, Herat**

Byron, *Road to Oxiana*, p. 88.
Babur, *Babur-Nama*, pp. 300, 303.
Babur, *op. cit.*, pp. 300, 303; Bretschneider, *Mediaeval Researches*, II, pp. 278–90; Byron, *op. cit.*, pp. 87–115; Le Strange, *Eastern Caliphate*, pp. 407–09; *Survey*, III, pp. 1130, 1141.
Biographical references are as follows: Ahmed ibn Arabshah, *Tamerlane*; Hookham, *Tamerlaine the Conqueror*; Timour[?], *Institutes*.

Plate 60, **Mausoleum of Gawhar Shad, Herat**

" Travel, Adventure and Sport," *Blackwood's Magazine*, VI (August 1885), pp. 130–31.
Byron, *Road to Oxiana*, pp. 100–01; Pope, *Persian Architecture*, p. 197; *Survey*, III, pp. 1128–29, 1134; Wilber, *Persian Gardens*, pp. 67–71. See also listings under Plate 59.

Plates 61-66, **Sanctuary of Abd Allah Ansari, Gazur Gah**

Persian Mystics: Invocations of Sheikh 'Abdullah Ansari of Herat, p. 37.
Byron, *Road to Oxiana*, pp. 105–06; *Encyclopedia of World Art*, I, pp. 39-40, 46-47; Pope, *Persian Architecture*, p. 198; *Survey*, III, pp. 1126, 1138–39. For discussions of faience technique, see Godard, *Art of Iran*, pp. 312–13, and Pope, *Persian Architecture*, pp. 165–67.

Plate 67, **View of Village near Khargird**

Arberry (ed.), *Hafiz: Fifty Poems*, p. 112.

Plates 68-69, **Masjid-i-Kali, Turbat-i-Shaykh Jam**

Wilber, *Islamic Iran*, p. 174.
Battuta, *Voyages*, III, pp. 74–77; Diez, *Churasanische Baudenkmäler*, pp. 78–82; Godard, *Art of Iran*, p. 293; Le Strange, *Eastern Caliphate*, pp. 357–58; *Survey*, III, pp. 1160–62, 1316; Wilber, *Islamic Iran*, p. 174.

Plates 70-74, **Madrasa, Khargird**

[1] *Survey*, III, p. 1127, note 1.
[2] *Ibid.*, p. 1135.
Athar-é Iran, IV, pp. 68–83; Diez, *Churasanische Baudenkmäler*, pp. 73–75; Diez, *D.K.d. islamischen Völker*, p. 100; *Encyclopedia of World Art*, VIII, p. 349; Herzfeld, *Archaeological History of Iran*, Plate XVII (for a plan); *Journal of the Royal Asiatic Society* (1910), p. 1149; Le Strange, *Eastern Caliphate*, pp. 357–58; Pope, *Persian Architecture*, pp. 197–98; *Survey*, III, pp. 1126–28, 1134–36, 1142.

Plates 75-78, **Blue Mosque, Tabriz**

[1] Herbert, *Some Yeares' Travels*, p. 195.
[2] Chardin, *Voyages*, I, p. 256.

Athar-é Iran, I, p. 69; Chardin, *op. cit.*, pp. 255–57; Coste, *Monuments modernes*, p. 54, Plate, LXVIII; Curzon, *Persian Question*, I, pp. 518–22; Dieulafoy, *Perse*, pp. 48–52; Flandin and Coste, *Voyage*, Plate V; Godard, *Art of Iran*, pp. 314–16; Jackson, *Persia*, pp. 43–44; Lockhart, *Famous Cities*, pp. 19–23; Minorsky, "Blue Mosque of Tabriz"; Pope, *Persian Architecture*, p. 203; Sarre, *Denkmäler*, p. 31; *Survey*, III, pp. 1130–31; Tavernier, *Les six voyages*, pp. 21–22; Texier, *Description de l'Arménie*, I, Plates XLII–LII; *ibid.*, II, pp. 48–50.

Chapter IV, **Safavid Period**; Plate 79, **Maidan, Isfahan**

[1] *Survey*, III, p. 1181.
[2] Herbert, *Some Yeares' Travels*, p. 156.
[3] Godard, in *Athar-é Iran*, II, p. 19.
Athar-é Iran, II, pp. 7–20, 103–07; Bellan, *Chah Abbas I*; Blunt and Swaan, *Isfahan*; Byron, *Road to Oxiana*, pp. 174–76; Chardin, *Voyages*, VII, pp. 334–43, Plates XXXIV–XXXV; Coste, *Monuments modernes*, p. 22, Plates VI–VIII; Curzon, *Persian Question*, II, pp. 20–41; Dieulafoy, *Perse*, p. 146; Jackson, *Persia*, pp. 262–70; Lockhart, *Fall of the Safavid Dynasty*; Lockhart, *Famous Cities*, pp. 14–18; Loti, *Vers Ispahan*, pp. 204–07; Speiser, *Oriental Architecture in Color*, pp. 113–33; *Survey*, III, pp. 1179–82, 1406–10; Sykes, *History of Persia*, II, p. 198; Valle, *Voyages*, II, p. 40; Wilber, *Persian Gardens*, pp. 79–119.

Plates 80-82, **Masjid-i-Shah, Isfahan**

Athar-é Iran, II, pp. 81–83, 107–16; *ibid.*, IV, pp. 309–10; Pope, " Representations of Living Forms in Persian Mosques, " pp. 125-29; Chardin, *Voyages*, VII, pp. 343–54; Coste, *Monuments modernes*, pp. 22-26, Plates VIII-XVII; Curzon, *Persian Question*, II, pp. 29–30; Flandin, *Relation du voyage*, I, pp. 343–48; Loti, *Vers Ispahan*, p. 208; Pope, *Persian Architecture*, pp. 210–17; Sarre, *Denkmäler*, pp. 78–79; *Survey*, III, pp. 1185–89; Sykes, *History of Persia*, II, p. 199; Tavernier, *Les six voyages*, p. 444; Texier, *Description de l'Arménie*, I, p. 163; *ibid.*, II, p. 133, Plates LXIX–LXXII; Valle, *Voyages*, II, p. 41.

Plates 83-87, **Masjid-i-Jami, Isfahan**

Survey, III, p. 1331. See also listings under Plates 9-16.

Plates 88-89, **Mausoleum of Harun-i-Vilaya, Isfahan**

Athar-é Iran, II, pp. 63–69; Chardin, *Voyages*, VII, pp. 450–54; Flandin and Coste, *Voyage*, Plate LXIII; Godard, *Art of Iran*, p. 318; Herzfeld, " Reisebericht," *Zeitschrift der deutschen morgenländischen Gesellschaft*, V (1926), 3, p. 238; Pope, *Persian Architecture*, p. 167; *Survey*, III, pp. 1170, 1331; Valle, *Voyages*, III, p. 45.

Plate 90, Darb-i-Kushk, Isfahan

[1] Wilber, *Persian Gardens*, p. 22.
Athar-é Iran, II, pp. 60-62; Saladin and Migeon, *Manuel*, I, p. 435; Sarre, *Denkmäler*, p. 77.

Plate 91, Chehel Sutun, Isfahan

[1] As quoted by Wilber, in *Persian Gardens*, p. 102.
Athar-é Iran, II, pp. 89–91, 116–20; Chardin, *Voyages*, VII, pp. 377–80; Coste, *Monuments modernes*, pp. 31–32, Plates XLI–XLIII; Dieulafoy, *Perse*, p. 132; Flandin, *Relation du voyage*, II, pp. 39–41; Gayet, *L'art persan*, pp. 184–88; Pope, *Persian Architecture*, p. 225; Sarre, *Denkmäler*, pp. 86–89, Plates LXVIII–LXIX; *Survey*, III, pp. 1192–93; Tavernier, *Les six voyages*, p. 527; Texier, *Description de l'Arménie*, I, p. 164, Plates LXXIII–LXXV; Wilber, *Persian Gardens*, pp. 100, 102.

Plate 92, Ali Kapu, Isfahan

[1] Herbert, *Some Yeares' Travels*, p. 156.
Athar-é Iran, II, pp. 80, 83–88; Bellan, *Chah Abbas I*, p. 75; Chardin, *Voyages*, VII, pp. 368, 386, 478; Dieulafoy, *Perse*, pp. 290–93; Flandin and Coste, *Voyage*, Plate LIX; Carson, "Ifsahan of Today," pp. 824–27; Sarre, *Denkmäler*, p. 83; *Survey*, III, pp. 1193–94; Tavernier, *Les six voyages*, pp. 443, 445, 475; Valle, *Voyages*, II, pp. 41, 46–50, 69–70; Wilber, *Persian Gardens*, pp. 37, 91–92.

Figures H-I; Plates 93-95, Hesht Behest, Isfahan

[1] Chardin, *Voyages*, VIII, p. 43.
Contarini, in *Travels to Tana and Persia*, pp. 133–34; Chardin, *op. cit.*, pp. 39–43; Coste, *Monuments modernes*, p. 30, Plates XXXVI–XL; Curzon, *Persian Question*, pp. 36–37; Pope, *Persian Architecture*, p. 231; Sarre, *Denkmäler*, p. 91; *Survey*, III, pp. 1195–97; Wilber, *Persian Gardens*, p. 107.

Plates 96-98, Masjid-i-Shaykh Lutfullah, Isfahan

[1] See Godard, *Art of Iran*, pp. 297–98 (for discussion of domes).
[2] Byron, *Road to Oxiana*, pp. 176–77.
Athar-é Iran, II, pp. 96–99; Byron, *op. cit.*, pp. 176–78; Chardin, *Voyages*, VII, pp. 354–60; Flandin, *Relation du voyage*, I, p. 349; Pope, *Persian Architecture*, pp. 217–18; Sarre, *Denkmäler*, pp. 79–82, Figure 104; *Survey*, III, pp. 1189–91; Tavernier, *Les six voyages*, p. 450; Valle, *Voyages*, II, p. 41.

Figure J; Plate 99, Chahar Bagh and Madrasa (by P. Coste); Madrasa Mader-i-Shah, Isfahan

Athar-é Iran, II, pp. 155–59; Coste, *Monuments modernes*, pp. 26–27, Plates XVIII–XXXI; Curzon, *Persian Question*, pp. 39–40; Dieulafoy, *Perse*, p. 142; Diez, *D.K.d. islamischen Völker*, pp. 106–07; Flandin, *Relation du voyage*, I, p. 352; Loti, *Vers Ispahan*,

pp. 221–27; Pope, *Persian Architecture*, p. 231; Sarre, *Denkmäler*, pp. 83–86, Figures 106–10; *Survey*, III, pp. 1213–15; Texier, *Description de l'Arménie*, I, p. 164, Plates LXXVI–LXXVIII; *ibid.*, II, pp. 137–39.

Plates 100-104, Seljuk Period Tomb Tower; Two Tomb Towers; Çifte Minareli Medrese, Erzurum

[1] Belin, "Extrait du journal," *Journal asiatique*, XIX, p. 377.
Belin, *op. cit.*, pp. 365–78; Clavijo, *Embassy*, p. 138; Diez, *D.K.d. islamischen Völker*, pp. 115, 122; Hill and Grabar, *Islamic Architecture*, p. 65, Plates CCCXXVIII–CCCXLI; Kinross, *Within the Taurus*, pp. 100–08; Le Strange, *Eastern Caliphate*, pp. 117–18; B. Lewis, *Istanbul*, pp. 12–16, 44–45; T. T. Rice, *Seljuks*, pp. 132, 141–42; Ünsal, *Turkish Islamic Architecture*, pp. 3, 4, 36–37, 46; Yetkin, *L'architecture turque*, pp. 22–28; Yetkin, "The Twin Minaret Medreseh," *Annales de l'Université d'Ankara*, IV (1954), pp. 255–59.

Plates 105-106, Mama Hatun Mausoleum, Tercan

Hill and Grabar, *Islamic Architecture*, Plates CCCXLII–CCCXLVIII; D. T. Rice, *Islamic Art*, p. 170, Plate CLXXI; T. T. Rice, *Seljuks*, p. 261, Plates XXIV–XXVI; Yetkin, *L'architecture turque*, pp. 22–28; Yetkin, "Mausoleum of Mama Hatun," *Burlington Magazine*, XCIX (May 1957), pp. 146–47.

Figure K, A Mongol Camp (by Friar Rubruquis)

[1] Friar Rubruquis, *Travels in Tartary and China*.

Plates 107-108, Ulu Cami, Eski Malatya

[1] Mustawfi, *Nozat-al-Kulub*, p. 162.
Arseven, *L'art turc*, pp. 30, 40–45; Hill and Grabar, *Islamic Architecture*, Plates CCCLXXVII–CCCLXXX; Le Strange, *Eastern Caliphate*, p. 120; T. T. Rice, *Seljuks*, p. 134; Ünsal, *Turkish Islamic Architecture*, p. 19; Yetkin, *L'architecture turque*, pp. 7–9.

Plates 109-112; Figure L, Sultan Han, Kayseri

[1] Gabriel, *Monuments turcs*, I, p. 99, Figure 64.
[2] W. H. Lewis, *Levantine Adventurer*, p. 58.
[3] Arseven, *L'art turc*, p. 62.
Arseven, *L'art turc*, pp. 62–63; Cholet, *Arménie*, pp. 66 ff.; Gabriel, *Monuments turcs*, pp. 93–100, Plates XXVIII–XXX; Jerphanion, *Mélanges*, pp. 92–102 (with photos and plans); E. Kühnel, in *Encyclopedia of World Art*, VIII, pp. 331, 351–353; Ramsey, *Historical Geography of Asia Minor*, p. 270; T. T. Rice, *Seljuks*, pp. 98–106; Sarre, *Denkmäler*, pp. 123–125; Sarre, *Reise in Kleinasien*, pp. 75 ff.; Taeschner, "Anatolische Forschungen," p. 114; Tozer, *Turkish Armenia*, pp. 167–68; Ünsal, *Turkish Islamic Architecture*, pp. 48, 50.

Plate 113, Countryside Between Tercan and Tunceli

Translated by Sir William Jones. From *The Works of Sir William Jones*, X, pp. 271–72.

Plate 114, Çifte Medrese, Kayseri

Gabriel, *Monuments turcs*, I, p. 62.
Diez, *D.K.d. islamischen Völker*, p. 120.
Le Strange, *Eastern Caliphate*, p. 146.
Arseven, *L'art turc*, pp. 44–45; Diez, *op. cit.*, pp. 117–20; Gabriel, *Monuments turcs*, I, pp. 60–62; Heyd, *Histoire du commerce du Levant*; Le Strange, *op. cit.*, pp. 142–46; Ottin, *Land of Emperors*, pp. 207–10, 219; T. T. Rice, *Seljuks*, pp. 98, 135; Saint-Pierre, *Trésors*, pp. 217–21; Ünsal, *Turkish Islamic Architecture*, p. 36. See also listings under Plate 115.

Plate 115, Huand Hatun Mausoleum, Kayseri

Gabriel, *Monuments turcs*, I, pp. 3–18 (on Kayseri generally), 39–52; Oberhummer and Zimmerer, *Durch Syrien*, p. 261; Sarre, *Reise in Kleinasien*, p. 127; Taeschner, "Anatolische Forschungen," p. 112; Texier, *Description de l'Asie Mineure*, II, pp. 58, 73, Plates LXXXVII–LXXXVIII; Tozer, *Turkish Armenia*, pp. 3 ff.; Ünsal, *Turkish Islamic Architecture*, p. 4. See also listings under Plate 114.

Plate 116, Sunghur Bey Mosque, Nigde

[1] See B. de Broquière, *Voyage d'outremer*, pp. 106, 109, 117 ff., regarding Moslem–Christian relations and labor importations.
Battuta, *Voyages*, II, pp. 285–86; Berchem, *Amida*, pp. 97, 99; Gabriel, *Monuments turcs*, I, pp. 123–35; Hammer-Purgstall, *Histoire de l'empire ottomane*, III, p. 116; Le Strange, *Eastern Caliphate*, pp. 142, 150; Lucas, *Deuxième voyage*, p. 182; Mustawfi, *Nozat-al-Kulub*, pp. 162–64; Texier, *Description de l'Asie Mineure*, II, p. 106.

Plates 117-118, Karatay Medrese, Konya

[1] Diez, *D.K.d. islamischen Völker*, p. 117.
Encyclopedia of World Art, XII, pp. 863–80; Huart, *Konia*; Kinross, *Within the Taurus*, pp. 174–81; Le Strange, *Eastern Caliphate*, pp. 145–46, 148–49; Löytved, *Konia*, pp. 45–51; T. T. Rice, *Seljuks*, pp. 138, 178–81; Sarre, *Denkmäler*, pp. 12, 127–30; Sarre, *Konia*, pp. 5–7, 11–14, Plates III–VIII; Sarre, *Reise in Kleinasien*, pp. 49–51, Plates XIX–XXI; Texier, *Description de l'Asie Mineure*, pp. 661–63; Ünsal, *Turkish Islamic Architecture*, pp. 31, 34, 106.

Plates 119-120, Sircali Medrese, Konya

[1] Wilber, *Islamic Iran*, p. 86.
Arseven, *L'art turc*, pp. 46–47, 53; Diez, *D.K.d. islami-*

schen Völker, p. 119; Gabriel, in *Encyclopedia of World Art*, X, p. 870; Gabriel, *Brousse*, I, pp. 89, 209; Kühnel, in *Encyclopedia of World Art*, VIII, pp. 331, 351–53; Löytved, *Konia*, pp. 42–44; Sarre, *Denkmäler*, text pp. 125–27, Plates (2nd ed.) pp. 9, 12; Sarre, *Konia*, pp. 10–12, Plates I–II; Sarre, *Reise in Kleinasien*, pp. 51–54, Plates XXII–XXV; Ünsal, *Turkish Islamic Architecture*, pp. 4, 30, 34.

Chapter VI, Ottomans: Bursa School

[1] Battuta, *Voyages*, II, p. 318.
[2] Belon, *Les observations*, pp. 450–51.
General references to Bursa and the Bursa style of Ottoman design are as follows: Arseven, *L'art turc*; Beaumont, "Voyage en Asie Mineure," *Revue orientale et algérienne*, I, pp. 478–92; II, pp. 65–85, 320–49; Belon, *op.cit.*; Cemal, *Bursa*; Diez, in *Islam Ansiklopedisi*, I, pp. 815–19; Gabriel, in *Encyclopedia of World Art*, X, pp. 855–59; Gabriel, *Brousse* (text and plates); Gavrilov, "Les corps de métiers," *Revue des études islamiques*, II (1928), pp. 207–30; Jouannin, "Souvenirs," *Bulletin de la Société de Géographie*, XI (1829), pp. 288–301; Loti, "La Mosquée Verte," *Revue de Paris*, I (July 15, 1894), pp. 225–45; Migeon and Sakisian, "La céramique d'Asie Mineure," *Revue de l'art ancien et moderne*, LXIII–LXIV (1923); Newberie, "Two Voyages," in Purchas, *His Pilgrims*, VIII, p. 475; Riefstahl, *Turkish Architecture*; Texier, *Description de l'Asie Mineure*, I, pp. 71–73, Plates XXII–XXVIII; Thévenot, *Relation d'un voyage*; Vogt-Göknil, *Turquie ottomane*; Wilde, *Brussa*; Yetkin, *L'architecture turque*.

Plates 121-124, Green Mausoleum, Bursa

[1] Godard, *Art of Iran*, pp. 262, 274 (discussion of the evolution of the mosque).
[2] Gabriel, *Brousse*, I, p. 99.
Arseven, *L'art turc*, pp. 143–44; Diehl, *Constantinople*, p. 100; Gabriel, *Brousse*, I, pp. 94–100, II, Plates XLI–XLIV; Mantran, "Inscriptions arabes," pp. 88–114; Ottin, *Land of Emperors*, pp. 237, 284; Parvillée, *Architecture et décoration turques*, Plates XXVIII–XLI; D. T. Rice, *Islamic Art*, pp. 184–85; Saint-Pierre, *Trésors*, pp. 221, 228, Plates CCVI–CCX; Taeschner, "Beiträge," pp. 145–46, 153–54; Vogt-Göknil, *Turquie ottomane*, pp. 49, 57–58; Yetkin, *L'architecture turque*, pp. 100–02.

Plates 125-128, Muradiye Mosque; Muradiye Medrese, Bursa

Arseven, *L'art turc*, p. 144; Babinger, *Mehmed*, p. 62; Diehl, *Constantinople*, pp. 98–99; Gabriel, *Brousse*, pp. 105–29, Plates XLVII–LXV; Mantran, "Inscriptions arabes," pp. 94, 109–10; Texier, *Description de l'Asie Mineure*, I, pp. 71–73, Plates XVII–XXII; Ünsal, *Turkish Islamic Architecture*, pp. 40, 47, 82; Wilde, *Brussa*, Figure 60; Yetkin, *L'architecture turque*, p. 104.

Chapter VII, **Ottomans: Istanbul Period**

[1] Letter to Mr. Derek Hill, quoted in Hill and Grabar, *Islamic Architecture*, p. 13.
References to stylistic differences between Byzantine and Ottoman are as follows: Gabriel, in *Encylopedia of World Art*, X, pp. 859–61; Gabriel, *Brousse*, pp. 207–11; Gabriel, *Turkey in Pictures*, Plates XI, XII, XIV, XVI, XVII; Speiser, *Oriental Architecture in Color*, pp. 160–77; Vogt-Göknil, *Turquie ottomane*, pp. 92–93 (plans of Sancta Sophia), p. 94 (drawing); Yetkin, "Evolution of Architectural Form," *Studia Islamica*, X-XIII (1959), pp. 73–91.

Plates 129-131, **Rustem Pasha Mosque, Istanbul**

[1] A great part of the information on Ottoman tiles has come from the scholarly work of Katharina Otto-Dorn (see below).
[2] Butler, *Islamic Pottery*.
Diehl, *Constantinople*, pp. 109–12; Edhem, *Nos mosquées de Stamboul*, pp. 89–90; Egli, *Sinan*, pp. 83–86; *Encyclopedia of World Art*, XIII, pp. 51–56; Gabriel, "Mosquées," pp. 389–90; Grosvenor, *Constantinople*, II, p. 662; Rice and Swaan, *Constantinople*, p. 157; Saint-Pierre, *Trésors*, p. 223; Ünsal, *Turkish Islamic Architecture*, pp. 27–28.
References to Ottoman tilework are as follows: Lane, "Ottoman Pottery," *Ars Orientalis*, II (1957); Migeon and Sakisian, "La céramique d'Asie Mineure," *Revue de l'art ancien et moderne*, XLIII–XLIV (1923); Otto-Dorn, *Das islamische Iznik*, pp. 109–64.

Plate 132, **Mihrimah Mosque, Istanbul**

Edhem, *Nos mosquées de Stamboul*, pp. 75–76; Egli, *Sinan*, pp. 61–63; Gabriel, "Mosquées," *Syria*, VII (1926), pp. 387–88; Grosvenor, *Constantinople*, II, p. 661; Vogt-Göknil, *Turquie ottomane*, p. 99, Plates CIX-CXVIII.

Plates 133-134, **Sokullu Mehmet Pasha Mosque, Istanbul**

Edhem, *Nos mosquées de Stamboul*, pp. 90–94; Egli, *Sinan*, pp. 98–101; Gabriel, "Mosquées," *Syria*, VII (1926), pp. 394–95, 403; Grosvenor, *Constantinople*, II,

pp. 418–19; Hürlimann, *Istanbul*, p. 107; Vogt-Gökni[l], *Turquie ottomane*, pp. 88 (plan), 102–03, Plates LXXVII[–]LXXXVI.
References to Koca Sinan are as follows: Arseve[n,] *L'art turc*, pp. 159–61, 212; Babinger, "Sinan [";] Corbett, "Sinan," *Architectural Review*, CXIII (Ma[y] 1953), pp. 291–97; Diehl, *Constantinople*, p. 104; Eg[li,] *Sinan*; Gabriel, in *Encyclopedia of World Art*, [X,] pp. 859–61; Gabriel, "Mosquées"; Grosvenor, *Constan[-]tinople*, II, pp. 418, 653, 667; Hürlimann, *Istanbu[l,]* pp. 46–48; B. Lewis, *Istanbul*, p. 78; Saint-Pierr[e,] *Trésors*, pp. 222–23; Ünsal, *Turkish Islamic Archite[c-]ture*, pp. 90–93; Vogt-Göknil, *Turquie ottoman[e,]* pp. 96–104.

Plate 135, **Mosque of Suleyman, Istanbul**

[1] Arseven, *L'art turc*, p. 212. The only paper so far foun[d] in the archives relating to plans of Sinan is a firman [of] 1567, in which the sultan gives his approval of the pla[n] and design presented to him by Sinan for the construc[-]tion of a room in the palace.
Arseven, *L'art turc*, pp. 163–67; Barth, *Constantinopl[e,]* pp. 136–40; Diehl, *Constantinople*, pp. 105–09; Edhem[,] *Nos mosquées de Stamboul*, pp. 83–84, Figures 39–40[;] Egli, *Sinan*, pp. 77–83; Gabriel, in *Encyclopedia o[f] World Art*, X, p. 860; Gabriel, *Turkey in Picture[s,]* Plates XLII–XLV; Gorsvenor, *Constantinople*, I[I,] pp. 666–72; Hürlimann, *Istanbul*, p. 98, Plates LII–LV[I;] Saint-Pierre, *Trésors*, pp. 222–23, 241–51; Speise[r,] *Oriental Architecture in Color*, pp. 80–83; Vogt-Gökni[l,] *Turquie ottomane*, pp. 17–18 (plan), 52–54, 99–10[1,] Plates XXXIII–XLIV.

Plates 136-138, **Sultan Ahmet Mosque, Istanbul**

[1] Busbeck, *Vier Briefe*, p. 32.
Arseven, *L'art turc*, pp. 171–74; Barth, *Constantinopl[e,]* p. 142; Diehl, *Constantinople*, pp. 113–15; Edhem, *N[os] mosquées de Stamboul*, pp. 116–17; Gabriel, in *Encyclo[-]pedia of World Art*, X, p. 862; Gabriel, "Mosquées[,"] p. 380; Gabriel, *Turkey in Pictures*, Plates XXV–XXV[I;] Grosvenor, *Constantinople*, II, pp. 676–84; Hürlimann[,] *Istanbul*, p. 70, Plates XXVII–XXXI; Speiser, *Orienta[l] Architecture in Color*, pp. 84–85; Yetkin, *L'architectur[e] turque*, pp. 128–30.

Bibliography

BBOTT, G. F. *Under the Turk in Constantinople: A Record of Sir John Finch's Embassy, 1674–81.* London, 1920.

HMED IBN ARABSHAH. *Tamerlane or Timur, the Great Amir,* ed. Sanders. London, 1936.

INSWORTH, W. F. *Travels and Research in Asia Minor.* London, 1842.

NHEGGER, R. *Beiträge zur frühosmanischen Baugeschichte.* Istanbul, 1953.

RBERRY, A. J. (ed.). *Hafiz: Fifty Poems.* Cambridge, 1962.

rs Islamica. Ann Arbor.

rs Orientalis. Ann Arbor.

RSEVEN, C. E. *L'art turc.* Istanbul, 1939.

——————. *Les arts décoratifs turcs.* Istanbul, 1950.

TABINEN, R. S. *Les caractéristiques de l'architecture turque.* Paris, 1938.

thar-é Iran. Journal published in Tehran. Godard was the prime contributor.

ABINGER, F. *Mehmed, der Eroberer und seine Zeit.* Munich, 1953.

——————. "Sinan," in *Encyclopedia of Islam.* Vol. IV, pp. 428–32. London, 1927.

ABUR PADSHAH GHAZI, ZAHIR U'D DIN MOHAMMED. *Babur-nama,* trans. Beveridge. London, 1921.

AHRAMI, M. "Le problème des ateliers d'étoiles de faïence lustrées," *Revue des arts asiatiques,* X (1937), 4.

——————. *Recherches sur les carreaux de revêtement lustré dans la céramique persane du XIIIᵉ au XVᵉ siècle.* Paris, 1937.

——————. "Some Examples of Il-Khanid Art," *Bulletin of the American Institute for Iranian Art and Archeology,* V (1938), pp. 257-60.

ARTH, H. *Constantinople.* Paris, 1906.

ATTUTA, IBN. *Voyages d'Ibn Batoutah,* trans. Defrémery and Sanguinetti. Paris, 1854.

EAUMONT, A. DE. "Voyage en Asie Mineure: Broussa," *Revue orientale et algérienne,* I, pp. 478–92; II, pp. 65–85, 320–49.

ELIN, R. "Extrait du journal d'un voyage de Paris à Erzeroum, 1852," *Journal asiatique,* Ser. 4, XIX, pp. 365–78.

BELLAN, L. L. *Chah Abbas I.* Paris, 1932.

BELON, P. *Les observations de plusieurs singularitez et choses mémorables trouvées en Grèce, Asie, Indée et autres pays étranges.* Paris, 1588.

BERCHEM, M. VAN. *Amida.* Heidelberg, 1910.

BLUNT, W., and SWAAN, W. *Isfahan, Pearl of Persia.* New York, 1966.

BRETSCHNEIDER, E. *Mediaeval Researches from Eastern Asiatic Sources.* London, 1910.

BROQUIÈRE, B. DE. *Voyage d'outremer,* ed. Schefer. Paris, 1892.

BROWNE, E. G. *A Year amongst the Persians.* London, 1950.

BUSBECK, O. G. VON. *Vier Briefe aus der Turkei,* ed. Steinen. Erlangen, 1926.

BUTLER, A. J. *Islamic Pottery.* London, 1926.

BYRON, R. *The Road to Oxiana.* London, 1950.

CAHEN, C. *Les seldjouks de Rum.* Brussels, 1950.

CARSON, B. "Ifsahan of Today," *Fortnightly Review,* CXXVI (December 1926), pp. 824-27.

CEMAL, A. *Bursa.* Istanbul, 1932.

CHARDIN, J. *Voyages du Chevalier Chardin en Perse et autres lieux de l'Orient,* ed. Langlès. Paris, 1811.

CHOLET, COMTE DE. *Arménie, Kurdestan et Mésopotamie.* Paris, 1892.

CLAVIJO, R. G. DE. *Embassy to Tamerlane,* trans. Le Strange. London, 1928.

CORBETT, S. "Sinan, Architect-in-Chief to Suleiman the Magnificent," *Architectural Review,* CXIII (May 1953), pp. 291–97.

COSTE, P. *Monuments modernes de la Perse.* Paris, 1867.

CRESWELL, K. A. C. *Early Muslim Architecture.* Oxford, 1932–40.

CURZON, G. N. *[Persian Question.] Persia and the Persian Question.* London, 1892.

CURZON, R. *Armenia.* London, 1854.

DIEHL, C. *Constantinople.* Paris, 1924.

DIEULAFOY, JANE. *La Perse, la Chaldée et la Susiane.* Paris, 1887.

DIEULAFOY, M. *L'art antique de la Perse.* Paris, 1884–85.

DIEZ, E. "Der Baumeister Sinan und sein Werk," *Atlantis,* XXV (April 1953), pp. 183–86.

——————. *Churasanische Baudenkmäler.* Berlin, 1918.

—————. *Iranische Kunst.* Vienna, 1944.

—————. [*D.K.d. islamischen Völker.*] *Die Kunst der islamischen Völker.* Berlin, 1918.

—————, and GLUCK, H. *Die Kunst des Islams.* Berlin, 1925.

EDHEM, H. *Nos mosquées de Stamboul,* trans. Mamboury. Istanbul, 1934.

EGLI, E. *Sinan, der Baumeister osmanischer Glanzzeit.* Stuttgart, 1954.

Encyclopedia of Islam. London, 1913–36.

Encyclopedia of World Art. New York, 1959–1967. (Articles on " Ilkhan Art," " Islam," " Ottoman Art," " Safavid Art," " Seljuk Art," and " Timurid Art.")

EVLIYA, E. *Narrative of Travels in Europe, Asia and Africa in the Seventeenth Century,* trans. Hammer. London, 1850.

FLANDIN, E. *Relation du voyage en Perse.* Paris, 1851.

—————, and COSTE, P. *Voyage en Perse.* Paris, 1851–54.

FLURY, S. " La Mosquée de Nayin, " *Syria,* XI (1930), pp. 43-58.

FRASER, J. B. [*Journey into Khorasan.*] *Narrative of a Journey into Khorasan in the Years 1821 and 1822.* London, 1825.

—————. *A Winter's Journey (Tatar) from Constantinople to Tehran, with Travels through Various Parts of Persia.* London, 1938.

FRYE, R. N. *The Heritage of Persia.* New York, 1963.

GABRIEL, A. [*Brousse.*] *Une capitale turque: Brousse–Bursa.* I, text; II, plates. Paris, 1958.

—————. *Les monuments turcs d'Anatolie.* Paris, 1934.

—————. " Les mosquées de Constantinople," *Syria,* VII (1926), pp. 353–419.

—————. *Turkey in Pictures.* London, 1962.

—————. *La Turquie orientale.* Paris, 1940.

GAVRILOV, M. " Les corps de métiers en Asie centrale et leurs statuts," *Revue des études islamiques,* II, (1928), pp. 207–30.

GAYET, A. *L'art persan.* Paris, 1895.

GLÜCK, H. *Die Kunst der Osmanen.* Leipzig, 1922.

GODARD, A. *Art of Iran.* New York, 1965.

—————. *Les monuments de Maragha.* (Société des études iraniennes et de l'art persan, publication IX.) 22 pages. Paris, 1934.

GREY, C. *A Narrative of Italian Travels in Persia.* (Hakluyt Society Series, Ser. 2, No. XLIX.) London, 1873.

GROSVENOR, E. A. *Constantinople.* Boston, 1899.

GRUBE, E. *The World of Islam.* New York, 1967.

HAMMER-PURGSTALL, J. *Histoire de l'empire ottoman.* Paris, 1835–43.

HELL, H. DE. *Voyage en Turquie et en Perse.* Paris, 1853–60.

HERBERT, SIR THOMAS. *Some Yeares' Travels into Divers Parts of Asia and Afrique.* London, 1638.

HERZFELD, E. *Archaeological History of Iran.* London, 1935.

—————. "Damascus: Studies in Architecture, I," *Ars Islamica,* IX (1942).

—————. *Iranische Denkmäler.* Berlin, 1932.

—————. " Reisebericht," *Zeitschrift der deutsch morgenländischen Gesellschaft,* V (1926), pp. 234–80.

HEYD, W. *Histoire du commerce du Levant au Moy Age.* Leipzig, 1936.

HILL, D., and GRABAR, O. *Islamic Architecture and Decoration.* London, 1964.

HOOKHAM, H. *Tamerlaine the Conqueror.* London, 196

HUART, C. *Konia: Ville des derviches tourneu* Paris, 1897.

HÜRLIMANN, M. *Istanbul.* London, 1958.

HUXLEY, J. *From an Antique Land.* London, 196

Islam Ansiklopedisi. Istanbul, 1943–60.

JACKSON, A. V. W. *Persia, Past and Present.* New Yo 1906.

JERPHANION, G. DE. *Mélanges d'archéologie anatolien* Beirut, 1928.

JONES, SIR WILLIAM. *The Works of Sir William Jon* Vol. X. London, 1807.

JOUANNIN, J. M. " Souvenirs d'un séjour à Brousse Bithynie dans l'année 1825," *Bulletin de Société de Géographie,* XI (1829), pp. 288–30

Journal of the Royal Asiatic Society. London.

KAI KA'US IBN ISKANDAR. [*Qabus Nama.*] *A Mirror Princes: The Qabus Nama,* trans. Lev New York, 1951.

KER PORTER, R. *Travels in Georgia, Persia, Armen Ancient Babylon . . . during the Years 18* *1818, 1819, 1820.* London, 1821.

KHOSRAU, NASSIRI. *Relation du voyage de Nass Khosrau,* trans. Schefer. Paris, 1881.

KINROSS, P. BALFOUR, BARON. *Within the Taur* New York, 1952.

LAMB, H. *Tamerlane, the Earth Shaker.* New York, 192

LANE, A. " Ottoman Pottery of Iznik," *Ars Oriental* II (1957).

LE STRANGE, G. [*Eastern Caliphate.*] *Lands of t Eastern Caliphate.* New York, 1966.

LEVY, R. " The Letters of Rashid al-Din Fadl-Allah *Journal of the Royal Asiatic Society,* I /II (194

LEWIS, B. *Istanbul and the Civilization of the Ottom Empire.* Norman, Oklahoma, 1963.

LEWIS, W. H. *Levantine Adventurer: The Travels a Missions of the Chevalier d'Arvieux, 1653–169* New York, 1963.

LOCKHART, L. *The Fall of the Safavid Dynasty.* Londo 1958.

—————. *Famous Cities of Iran.* London, 193

LOTI, P. " La Mosquée Verte," *Revue de Paris,* (July 15, 1894), pp. 225–45.

—————. *Vers Ispahan.* Paris, n.d.

LÖYTVED, J. H. *Konia: Inschriften der seldschukische Bauten.* Berlin, 1907.

LUCAS, P. *Deuxième voyage.* Paris, 1712.

LUTYENS, E. " Persian Brickwork, II," *Country Lif* LXXIII (February 4, 1933), pp. 118–23.

MacLEAN, F. *Eastern Approaches.* London, 1949.

MacNEILL, W. H. *The Rise of the West.* Chicago, 196

MANTRAN, R. " Inscriptions arabes de Brousse, *Bulletin d'études orientales de l'Institut França de Damas,* XIV (1952–54), pp. 88–114.

—————. *La vie quotidienne à Constantinople a temps de Soliman le Magnifique.* Monaco, 196

AYER, L. A. *Islamic Architects and Their Works.* Geneva, 1956.

GEON, G., and SAKISIAN, A. " La céramique d'Asie Mineure et de Constantinople du XIVᵉ au XVIIIᵉ siècle," *Revue de l'art ancien et moderne,* XLIII–XLIV (1923).

INORSKY, V. "The Blue Mosque of Tabriz," *East of Islam,* IV. Leiden /London, 1927, pp. 583–93.

————. " Maragha," in *Encyclopedia of Islam.* Vol. III. London, 1936.

————. " The Mosque of Varamin," *Apollo,* XIII (1931), pp. 155–58.

ORIER, J. *A Journey through Persia, Armenia and Asia Minor to Constantinople, in the Years 1808 and 1809.* London, 1812.

————. *A Second Journey through Persia, Armenia and Asia Minor to Constantinople, between the Years 1810 and 1816.* London, 1818.

USTAWFI, H. A. *Nozat-al-Kulub.* Bombay, 1894.

EWBERIE, J. "Two Voyages of Master John Newberie," in *Purchas, His Pilgrims,* ed. Samuel Purchas. Glasgow, 1905.

BERHUMMER, R., and ZIMMERER, H. *Durch Syrien und Kleinasien.* Berlin, 1899.

LEARIUS, A. *Muskowitische und persische Reyse.* Schleswig, 1654.

————. *Relation du voyage de Adam Olearius en Muscovie, Tartarie et Perse.* Paris, 1866.

MAR KHAYYAM. *Rubaiyat,* trans. Fitzgerald. New York, 1952.

TTIN, M. *Land of Emperors and Sultans.* New York, 1964.

TTO-DORN, K. *Das islamische Iznik.* Berlin, 1941.

ARVILLÉE, L. *Architecture et décoration turques au XVᵉ siècle.* Paris, 1874.

ersian Mystics: Invocations of Sheikh 'Abdullah Ansari of Herat, trans. J. Singh. (Wisdom of the East Series.) New York, 1939.

OPE, A. U. *[North Dome.] Note on the Aesthetic Character of the North Dome of the Masjid-i-Jami of Isfahan.* Cairo, 1965.

————. *Persian Architecture.* New York, 1965.

————. " Persian Brickwork," *Country Life,* LXXII (December 31, 1932), pp. 742–47.

————. " Representations of Living Forms in Persian Mosques, " *Bulletin of the Iranian Institute of America,* VI /VII (December 1946), pp. 125–29.

AMSEY, W. *Historical Geography of Asia Minor.* London, 1896.

RICE, D. T. *Islamic Art.* New York, 1965.

————, and SWAAN, W. *Constantinople.* New York, 1965.

RICE, T. T. *The Seljuks in Asia Minor.* London, 1961.

RIEFSTAHL, R. M. *Turkish Architecture in Southwestern Anatolia.* Cambridge, Mass., 1931.

ROSS, E. D. " The Tatars: Early History of the Seljuks," *Royal Central Asian Society,* XV (1928), pp. 136–41.

RUBRUQUIS, FRIAR. *Travels in Tartary and China in 1253,* ed. de Bergeron. The Hague, 1735.

SAINT-PIERRE, M. DE. *Trésors de la Turquie.* Paris, 1959.

SALADIN, H., and MIGEON, G. *Manuel de l'art musulman.* Vol. I, Paris, 1907.

SARRE, F. *Denkmäler persischer Baukunst.* Berlin, 1901–10.

————. *Konia: Seldschukische Baudenkmäler.* Berlin, 1910.

————. *Reise in Kleinasien.* Leipzig, 1894.

————. *Seldschukische Kleinkunst.* Leipzig, 1909.

————, and HERZFELD, E. *Archäologische Reise im Euphrat- und Tigris-Gebiet.* Berlin, 1911-20.

SCHROEDER, E. " Preliminary Note on Work in Persia and Afghanistan," *Bulletin of the American Institute of Persian Art and Archaeology,* IV (1936), pp. 134–35.

SHERLEY, A., SHERLEY, R., and SHERLEY, T. *The Three Brothers: Or the Travels and Adventures of Sir Anthony, Sir Robert and Sir Thomas Sherley in Persia, Russia, Turkey, Spain....* London, 1825.

SMITH, M. B., and SMITH, K. " Islamic Monuments of Iran," *Asia,* XXXIX (1939), 4, pp. 213–16.

SPEISER, W. *Oriental Architecture in Color.* New York, 1965.

STERN, S. M. " Inscriptions of the Kharraqan Mausoleums," *Iran,* IV (1966), pp. 21–27.

STEVENS, R. *Land of the Great Sophy.* London, 1962.

STRONACH, D., and YOUNG, C. " Three Seljuk Tomb Towers," *Iran,* IV (1966), pp. 1–6, 16–20, Figures 2–4, Plates I–VI.

————, " 11th–Century Seljuk Tombs Discovered in Western Iran," *Illustrated London News* (September 25, 1965), pp. 38–39.

STUART, C. *Journal of a Residence in Northern Persia.* London, 1854.

[Survey.] Survey of Persian Art, ed. Pope, *et al.* 13 vols. Tokyo, 1965.

SYKES, SIR P. *History of Persia,* London, 1958.

TAESCHNER, F. " Anatolische Forschungen," *Zeitschrift der deutschen morgenländischen Gesellschaft,* LXXXII (1928), p. 114.

————. " Beiträge zur frühosmanischen Epigraphik und Archäologie," *Islam,* XX (1932), pp. 145–46, 153–54.

TAVERNIER, J. B. *The Six Voyages of Jean-Baptiste Tavernier through Turkey into Persia and the East Indies.* London, 1678.

————. *Les six voyages en Turquie, en Perse, et aux Indes.* Paris, 1681.

THÉVENOT, J. DE. *Relation d'un voyage fait au Levant.* Paris, 1665.

————. *Travels of Monsieur de Thévenot into the Levant.* London, 1687.

TIMUR [authenticity questionable.] *Institutes, Political and Military,* ed. White, trans. Davy. London, 1780.

TOZER, H. F. *Turkish Armenia and Eastern Asia Minor.* London, 1883.

" Travel, Adventure and Sport," *Blackwood's Magazine,* VI (August 1885), pp. 130–31.

Travels to Tana and Persia (15th Century). (Hakluyt

Society Series, Ser. 1, No. XLIX.) New York, 1964.

ÜNSAL, B. *Turkish Islamic Architecture*. London, 1959.

VALLE, P. DELLA. *Voyages de P. della V[alle] dans la Turquie, l'Egypte, la Palestine, la Perse, les Indes Orientales, et autres lieux*. Paris, 1745.

VOGT-GÖKNIL, U. *Les mosquées turques*. Zurich, 1953.

WHITE, J. *Timur*. [1st ed., 1783.] London, 1963.

WILBER, D. N. "The Development of Mosaic Faience in Islamic Architecture in Iran," *Ars Islamica*, VI (1939), pp. 16–47.

——————. *Iran, Past and Present*. Princeton, 1948.

——————. *[Islamic Iran.] The Architecture of Islamic Iran: The Il Khanid Period*. Princeton, 1955.

——————. *Persian Gardens and Garden Pavilions*. Tokyo, 1962.

WILDE, H. *Brussa*. Berlin, 1909.

WILSON, A. T. "Some Early Travelers in Persi *Journal of the Central Asia Society*, XII (192 pp. 68–92.

WITTEK, P. *The Rise of the Ottoman Empire*. (Ro Asiatic Society Monographs, No. XXI London, 1936.

YETKIN, S. K. *L'architecture turque en Turquie*. Pa 1962.

——————. "Evolution of Architectural Form Turkish Mosques, 1300–1700," *Studia Is mica*, X-XIII (1959), pp. 73–91.

——————. "Mausoleum of Mama Hatun," *Burli ton Magazine*, XCIX (May 1957), pp. 146–

——————. "The Twin Minaret Medreseh Erzurum," *Annales de l'Université d'Anka IV (1954), pp. 255–59.*